"There I was at 500 Feet…."

An anecdotal history of
No 1 Parachute Training School
1940 – 1990

Peter Hearn BA, AFC, RAF (R'td)

with

Haydn Welch

Copyright © 2024 Haydn Welch

All rights reserved.

ISBN: 9798434908863

DEDICATION

To Ken 'Joe' Welch
and
Ian 'Mac' McGregor, Jim 'Ginger' Averis, Edgar 'Natch' Markwell
("The Four Toffs")

Peter Hearn for collecting the anecdotal stories from fellow Parachute Jump Instructors without whom this book would have little purpose.

Julie Hearn for permission to reproduce her father's work in this volume.

For all those who jumped

The author has attempted to credit the artist of the Top Spot cartoon depicting Louis Strange in his Martinsyde. Should the copyright holder wish to contact me, I will ensure the correct acknowledgment appears in future printings of this book. If other images are not correctly credited, please contact me haydnwelch@outlook.com

ACKNOWLEDGEMENTS

I acknowledge all the contributors whose anecdotes appear in this volume. Ken's wife Denise and my sister Lorie Randall (Lorna Welch) for her research and contributions which has led to some corrections and additions in this work. What started as a request for a couple of anecdotes lead on to telling a much bigger story. I couldn't help it.

Ken 'Joe' Welch

CONTENTS

Foreward

Preface

Introduction

PART ONE

1. Ringway - The Early Years   Pg 07
2. Ringway - The Later Years   Pg 27
3. Middle East PTS   Pg 51
4. Far East PTS India   Pg 74
5. Upper Heyford   Pg 81
6. Abingdon 1950-1965   Pg 87
7. Abingdon 1965-1975   Pg 104
8. Brize Norton   Pg 117
9. 1990 and Beyond   Pg 126

PART TWO

10. Haydn   Pg 131
11. Ken   Pg 140
12. Who's the Daddy?   Pg 142
13. Back to Ken   Pg 147
14. Haydn & Lorna   Pg 159
15. The PJIs   Pg 219
16. Further Reading   Pg 221
17. About the Authors   Pg 222

FOREWARD

Part One of this volume is a faithful copy of Peter's original work "There I was at 500 feet". Along with a few additions and observations which Haydn has made. He has also included all of the images throughout.

Part Two tells a little of what became of just one of these Parachute Jump Instructors after the war, Haydn's dad. Particularly how it was for Haydn and his sister Lorna in having a father such as Ken.

I hope you enjoy your dive into the daring world of the RAF Parachute Jump Instructor and let these tales collected by Peter elevate your spirit. I hope they inspire you as you experience the anecdotal history of the RAF Parachute Training School.

I hope you are captivated by chronicles of the remarkable stories of the men who taught the men to jump. From exhilarating first jumps to heartwarming moments of the airborne soldier, these stories capture the thrill, humour, and humanity behind each leap.

Reflect on the impact of Ken's wartime profession as he trained the troops to experience the heart-pounding excitement of leaping from an aeroplane, knowing in a coming day they would jump into battle.

Let history meet adrenaline and discover the profound legacy of being a child of one such PJI. Follow Haydn, as he navigates a childhood filled with adventure, challenges, and unique lessons learned from a father who was happier at 500 feet than he was at home.

A father whose values and resilience transcended the drop zone and instilled lessons of courage and discipline, as Haydn captures the essence of growing up with a parent whose life was defined by unwavering commitment to military adventure above the deserts of North Africa.

With each story I hope you will gain insight into the camaraderie, courage, and life lessons that unfold in the skies. The resilience and bravery shared through exhilarating experience.

How Ken shaped Haydn's values, inspired his dreams, and prepared him for life's challenges, on the ground, at sea and in the air.

From lessons learned in the face of adversity, this book celebrates the profound influence of a father who taught his son to reach for the skies. The journey of discovering his own place amidst the legacy of a man who wore a parachute to work. A man who experienced the glory above the clouds which would resonate far beyond the airfield.

How Haydn's life was entangled with a flavour of his dad's spirit from birth. The highs and lows of growing up in the shadow of a legend who showed how the sky is not the limit, but just the beginning. As Ken taught Haydn to navigate the lessons he had learned in the heat of the desert.

Start your journey today and uncover the legacy of the PJIs where bravery and history take flight. Where every jump tells a story and every story inspires a leap of faith. I hope they kindle sparks of adventure in you as they do for Haydn and once did for his dad.

Nicola Welch

PREFACE

I met Peter at Dad's funeral in 2007. We spoke of stories Dad had told me over the years. I never tired of asking him to tell them again. He never tired of telling. Now Peter was telling them and they were so familiar. Peter of course had a few more to tell and it seemed he too would not tire of telling.

We spoke of Dad's last few years where I had suggested he should make just one more jump. A tandem skydive, I would arrange four generations of our family to jump with him, in the same patch of sky, all at the same time. It would be Dad's swansong. It didn't happen. Dad did not want one last jump.

A couple of years later I tried again to rekindle Dad's outrageous spirit for adventure. This time to get him awarded a Guiness World Record as the World's oldest wing walker. The opportunity presented itself at Dunkeswell, my local airfield, from where I made most of my jumps and latterly from where I flew my Goldwing microlight. Dad listened to the plan but again refused.

This was the man who went "three good rounds" with Bruce Woodcock, who at the time, was the British ABA champion and would become the heavyweight champion of the British Empire. He was the man who in 1943 commandeered a freefall parachute and persuaded a Canadian pilot to go around one more time a little higher so he could jump for fun. The man who taught the SAS to jump and who dispatched Colonel David Stirling on that fateful stormy night which saw the loss of so many valiant souls during Operation Squatter. The man who spent the rest of the war getting up to mischief with the SAS and the LRDG in the deserts of North Africa.

Sometime later, Dad came to see me. He had spoken with fellow 'Middle East Toff' Jim Averis (Ian and Natch having previously passed away), they would both do the wing walk. Dad would go first and get the World Record. Jim would then go, and being three years older, get the record off Dad.

Sadly, a few weeks later, his friend the old Toff died and the wing walk lost its purpose.

I said to Peter, that such stories would make a great book. Peter went to his car and retrieved a copy of an old typewritten manuscript, which many years earlier he had given to a few PJIs at a Canopy Club reunion. He pressed it into my hand and said these would help to start it off.

After Peter died, I messaged Peter's daughter Julie and we agreed it would be a lovely tribute to publish these tales in their entirety, rather than seeing a few of them picked out and appearing randomly in any number of works. These then are the tales that turned people into legends.

Haydn Welch

INTRODUCTION

This collection of personal reminiscences by Parachute Jumping Instructors, and friends, is not intended to be a complete nor necessarily accurate history of the Parachute Training School. These are the tales of the crew room. These are the stories one hears at reunions of the PTS Canopy Club, or wherever two or more PJIs get together. This is the folklore of the Parachute Training School, not its definitive history. I suggest that its main value to the historian lies in the collective portrayal of a sense of humour and a tendency to modest understatement that marks the PJI and when the airborne soldier puts on his parachute for real and goes to war.

On the basis that this is a collection of folklore, editing of contributions has been kept to a minimum. Apart from a small amount of standardisation or omission of those comments that might have contravened either the Official Secrets Act or the laws of libel, the words are those of the PJI as given to, or borrowed by me. I have provided a linking commentary, which I have kept as brief as possible.

Most contributions have been given to me specifically for this booklet. A few I have lifted from official reports. Others I have drawn from previously written reminiscences, notably those of Louis Strange, for which I thank his daughter, Professor Susan Selly. Of Maurice Newnham, whose contributions I have taken from his book 'Prelude to Glory'. Of Bill Jevons who wrote an excellent paper on the early history of PTS and of Harry Ward, whose contributions are taken from his autobiography 'The Yorkshire Birdman'. I have also drawn from material given to me many years ago for my book 'Parachutist'. To bring the work right up to date, I have included a selection of choice comments from the current PTS Line Book.

To all those who have helped put together these fifty years of PTS folklore, I offer thanks on behalf of those who will no doubt enjoy the result.

Peter Hearn

Bless 'em all, bless 'em all
The parachute packers and all
Bless all the Sergeants and their paratroops
Bless all the packers and their statichutes
'Cos we're saying goodbye to them all
As out of the Whitleys we fall
You'll get no promotion if your 'chute doesn't open
So cheer up, my lads, bless 'em all.

PART ONE

1 RINGWAY – THE EARLY YEARS

We ought to have a corps of at least 5,000 parachute troops. Pray let me have a note from the War Office on the subject.
Winston Churchill to the Chiefs of Staff, 6th June 1940

As a result of that directive, it was decided to form a Central Landing Establishment at Manchester's airport, Ringway. Appointed to set up a parachute training unit as part of that centre were Major John Rock of the Royal Engineers, and Squadron Leader Louis Strange.

He was already somewhat of a legendary character in the RAF. As a combat fighter in the first war, he won the DSO, MC and DFC and reached the rank of Lieutenant Colonel in the Royal Flying Corps. When the RAF was formed in 1918, he was appointed Wing Commander and Chief Instructor at the Central Flying School at Upavon. He left the service in 1922 to take up civil flying.

In September 1940, he entered the Air Force for the second time, and very soon gained a bar to his DFC. During the retreat across France, he ferried a plane over the Channel and landed on an airfield which was already receiving attention from the enemy. Streams of allied troops hurrying towards the coast warned him that the enemy were rapidly approaching. He succeeded in taking off two Hurricanes which were lying on the field, un-serviced and dangerously short of fuel, and flying them back to England. Strange had never flown a Hurricane in his life, and all the instruments were out of order. "I wouldn't have understood them if they had been working," he said afterwards…

The same qualities of daring and initiative which brought him back from France in two wars were now devoted to building up a school for training paratroops. He had a happy knack of leadership, an impatient contempt for slow official channels, and next to no knowledge of parachuting. One experience in 1915, however, had made him decidedly parachute conscious. While flying a Martinsyde over enemy lines, he stood up in the cockpit in an endeavour to change a Lewis gun drum. The next moment, he found himself hanging onto the drum by his hands while the plane was flying upside down above him. Happily for him, the drum was well and truly jammed. He let go with one hand and managed to swing a leg far enough inside the cockpit to work the stick with his feet, and turn the plane over.

Bill Jevons

Drawing from the 1959 *Top Spot* cartoon

That was before aircrew had parachutes! Actually, Louis Strange, who was only a Pilot Officer in 1940, was not initially posted to Ringway to command the proposed school, but as a member of its staff. Squadron Leader Ross Shore was nominated as CO, but broke his ankle making a jump at Henlow before he ever arrived at Ringway. Louis Strange tells the story of how he came to command the school...

My posting and those of the others selected from 24 Squadron as aircrew for the new Parachute Training School came through on 23rd June, and we all flew up to Ringway and reported on the 24th. The Station Commander, Wing Commander Blackford, had not been fully informed as yet of the aims and objects of the School, so we were unable to do much about it, having no aircraft or equipment. On the 27th, Captain J F Rock arrived with 50 soldiers. This was the first clue that we had as to the nature of the work expected of PTS. Seeing that there was no time to be lost, I took it upon myself to go up to the Air Ministry and see what I could find out. Wing Commander Sir Nigel Norman kindly lent me a Leopard Moth for the trip, and I flew from Ringway to Hendon on June 29th.

I at last found that PTS came under the Director of Combined Operations. Having found that DCO Air - Group Captain Bowman - I explained what was going on, or rather, not going on, at Ringway, and then learnt about Ross Shaw's accident. Bowman was at that very time urgently requesting a replacement from Postings Air Ministry. After a good deal of telephoning without any result, he presently gave up the unequal struggle, lent back in his chair and said "Here, Louis", (we were old friends) "You'll have to take this job on, we can't wait any longer. Go out and get your tailor to put a stripe on either side of the one you've got, and meet me for lunch. I'll have to tell Postings if they won't tell me." Never were two stripes added to a VR's tunic more rapidly or less deserved.

Louis Strange

Louis Strange's next stop was to RAF Henlow

Next day I flew to Henlow, the home of parachutes. The experimental section had already modified an experimental Whitley bomber, and by removing the lower fuselage gun turret, commonly known as the 'dust-bin', had made an aperture large enough for a man's body to drop through. The Station Commander agreed to lend me Flight Lieutenant Miles, Flying Officer Powell and ten airmen who had volunteered as instructors in the new school.

The very next day Powell took them over to Bassingbourne where under Miles' direction they all made a successful jump. A/C Oakes was the first to go, and he landed on the Station fire tender, which was standing by the waiting ambulance, quite unhurt, the remainder landed on or near the aerodrome. Their names, which should never be lost to Air Force or Airborne history, are as follows: Terry Oakes, Paddy Gavin, Bill Pacey, Kim Campbell, Lofty Humphries, Frankie Chambers, Taff Roberts, Bill Walton, Padddy Wicklow, Harry Harwood.

Louis Strange

Louis Strange

Harry Ward, one of the earliest of the Ringway Pioneers, has fond memories of Louis Strange...

Louis Strange was a marvelous man to work for. No time at all for 'bull' and red tape. When they decided to jump through the hole in the Whitley instead of being dragged one at a time from the rear platform, he went straight to Armstrong Whitworth's to arrange for the modifications to be made to the fuselages of our kites. By the time the Air Ministry heard of it and complained about irregular procedures, the 'hole' was already in use.

Harry Ward

Rear exit from a Whitley

With the first pupils due to arrive on 9th July, Louis Strange looked for a suitable dropping zone…

Nigel Norman first spotted Tatton Park, the home of Lord Egerton, five miles from Ringway, and we at once decided it was by far the most suitable site in the locality. The Army, The War Agricultural Committee and another branch of the RAF were all after Tatton Park, but we pleaded our cause with Lord Egerton (himself a pioneer aviator) to such good effect that from the word 'go' he gave us every possible support, assistance and encouragement. We cut down his trees, we knocked down his gate posts, we landed all over his park. He himself, his tenants and farm laborers, the cattle, sheep and horses, were in danger of having a paratrooper land on their backs. Yet I cannot remember Lord Egerton ever having any complaints to make. To his co-operation in those days I attribute a very great deal of the early success of PTS. It was, I think, inspired a little from the fact that this open space and the large wooden building on it was his own aerodrome and hanger, from which he flew his own aeroplane as far back as 1909 and 1910.

Louis Strange

On 11th July, the first dummies were dropped at Tatton. By this time, the staff had been augmented by a real live parachutist – pilot Officer Williams – who in peace time had thrilled crowds at Air Circus displays. With him to advise and encourage, the instructors prepared to make their first descents. Watched by the Army instructors and 100 Commando pupils, the eight RAF fabric workers showed how easy it was. Two of them did 'lift off' descents from the edge of the gaping hole in the floor and launched themselves into space. The next day the Army instructors and Major Rock tried it for themselves.

Bill Jevons

One of those Army instructors was Sergeant Johnny Dawes…

We fitted our 'chutes', the old training type, with the pack at the back and ripcord in front. RSM Manzie was No 1. I was No 2, FS Brereton was our dispatcher.

We took off and the Sergeant Major crawled through the hatch on to the platform which was fitted inside the turret. FS Brereton crouched beside him, watching the ground. With hand upraised ready to give him the signal to pull the ripcord. I saw No 1 hanging on grimly to the cross-bar of the turret, staring at me with glassy eyes, then suddenly there was a flash of white and he had gone. Very gingerly I crawled aft and took his place, taking great pains not to look down. FS Brereton shouted in my ear. "Take your time. We'll make a dummy run first and you can drop on the second run. We are almost over Tatton Park now."

With great effort of will I dared to look down on my first bird's eye view of the English countryside. To my horror I saw five hundred feet below a tiny stretcher with a dark motionless figure being lifted into a blood-wagon. FS Brereton must have seen it too, for he looked hard at me and said, "There's nothing to worry about. If you like, I'll pull the ripcord for you myself."

"I'm alright," I said, clutching the bar feverishly. "Just tell me what to do."

"Watch my hand then, and when you see it fall, pull the handle upward and outward."

"Okay," I said. "You mean like this…?"

"Not now you bloody fool …!"

But it was too late, I'd gone! Three hours later the search party found me, six miles away from the dropping zone, hanging helplessly from the highest branches of a clump of trees.

Johnny Dawes

That figure on the stretcher had been Sergeant Major Manzie, suffering a serious concussion! More expertise was added to the staff with the arrival at Ringway of two more 'circus' jumpers to join Pilot Officer Bruce Williams. Harry Ward recalls …

Bruce had joined up in 1939, had been trained as an air-gunner, had been shot down in a Defiant over the Channel in early 1940, and had come out of hospital just in time for Louis Strange to pick him up for the Ringway job. It was Bruce Williams who would produce much of the ground training equipment – including the 'fan' – that others would later get the credit for.

While my posting to Ringway was being arranged, Bruce had

gone in search of Bill Hire. All three of us used to jump together for the same Air Circus. He found him running a London dancehall, a number which Bill was rather loath to give up, even for a direct Commission into the RAF. Bruce told him that if he didn't take it, he'd probably finish up in an Army cookhouse when his call came through, and that appealed to Bill even less, so he joined us. There we were, the three circus pro's, all set to teach the British Army to become parachutists. Moreover, who should be in command of the three Whitleys, but Flight Lieutenant Earl B Fielden, with whom I had shared four happy circus tours when he was piloting the old Argosy!

But this was a very different circus. Bruce, Bill and I may have been experienced show-jumpers, but the delivery of troops to battle was a very different kettle of fish. Everybody, including ourselves, was starting from scratch. No suitable transport aircraft; no parachute designed for airborne delivery; no training system; no previous knowledge of airborne practice and theory. Just a band of Army PTIs, RAF parachute workers, a former RFC pilot, three ex-circus pro's, and three clapped out Whitley bombers under the command of a former circus flier – that was how the training of Britain's airborne forces began.

That initial bunch of trainees at the Parachute School – the men of No 2 Commando – were a hard bunch, but some of them were not hard enough. Although all were volunteers for parachute training, when they came face to face with the reality of it, 30 of those 342 were unable to pitch themselves through that hole in the floor of the Whitley. Not surprisingly. It was a diabolical system, and the accident rate was high in those early days. Two more men died before the end of 1940 (the first had been Driver Evans, in July) and there were far too many bods limping around on crutches or wearing battered faces that were the reward for 'ringing the bell'. Yes, it was a hard business, and those types who pioneered it without benefit of previous parachuting experience deserve the highest praise.

Harry Ward

There were lighter moments, Harry recalls ...

Despite the dangerous and serious nature of the job - or perhaps because of it – there was plenty of fun to be had at Ringway in those early days. I suppose that we ex-circus types brought a certain irreverence into the military atmosphere. One thing we didn't like was parading. Wing Commander Strudwick, who was the Station CO, loved it. He insisted that all officers and men should attend a full Station parade every Saturday morning. Not if we could help it! Bill Hire and I suddenly discovered a pressing need to carry out a close investigation of deployment curve of the 'X' type parachute as used from the Whitley. At least, that's what we told Strudwick. We explained that much as we would regret having to miss the Station parade, the only time that we could carry out these trials without disrupting normal training was on Saturday mornings. We had willing allies amongst the crews, so every Saturday Mac Monnies would wind up the Whitley, Bob Fender fly the Hawker Hind with Lawrence Wright on the camera, and Bob Hire and I would lob out over Tatton Park, to be collected by jeep and taken to a cosy little café at Knutsford for the rest of the morning.

Harry Ward

Amongst some of the first of many foreign troops to be trained at Ringway were the Poles. Some had previous experience of military parachuting, Poland having being one of the few nations to have followed the example of the Russian airborne pioneers in the 1930s ...

Among them was Flying Officer Julien Gebolys whose transition from the role of pupil to instructor was unusually rapid. He arrived in March 1941 with a party of Polish Army officers. After hearing the customary address of welcome by the CO, they proceeded to the synthetic training area under the expert eye of FS Brereton, and their first period was spent in learning how to control a parachute. Almost immediately Gebolys entered into an argument with his instructor, politely but firmly implying in his charming Polish accent that the Flight Sergeant was wrong — as if a FS could be!
"Who are you anyway, and what do you know about it?"
"I was an instructor in parachuting for fife years, and haf done sefenty four jumps."
"You'd better report to the Chief Instructor," said FS Brereton somewhat shaken — and Gebolys told his story again in Flt Lt Ward's office.

"You go back," said the Chief Instructor, "And take over the section …"

Julien's record reads like a war time thriller. Before he became one of Poland's first parachute instructors in 1936 he was a pilot in the Polish Air Force. He supervised the construction of 24 jumping towers on the lines of those used by the Russian parachute clubs. When the Germans over-ran Poland he hid in civilian clothing in Warsaw for 4 months until he was warned that the Gestapo were on his track. With the help of the Polish underground he was smuggled into Russia, then by devious routes into Sweden and France. When France fell, he escaped to North Africa then to Gibraltar, and finally reached England in December 1940.

Bill Jevons

Julien Gebolys was to drop into Arnhem in 1944 as Liaison Officer with the Polish Brigade. Another officer to arrive at Ringway in 1941 was Charles Agate. He too experienced Harry Ward's disbelief in extensive preparation for the job …

Charles Agate had been a PT teacher before joining the RAF and being trained as an air-gunner. He had been posted to duties as a ground instructor, which didn't appeal to him. He had read about the Italian raid (*the raid on the Tragino Aquaduct in March 1941*) and the existence of a Parachute Training School, and applied for a transfer to parachuting duties, which sounded more exciting than gunnery instruction.

When he reported in his best uniform to Louis Strange, the boss chatted to him for a few minutes, then sent him to me for training.

"You're in luck," I said. "we've got a kite going off for a dropping sortie in a few minutes."
I had him fitted with an 'X' type, and out on board a Whitley with its engines already running. A few minutes later, over Tatton Park and still wearing his best uniform, he jumped No 1 ahead of seven Norwegian troops. He has been at Ringway almost an hour. Nothing like the 'deep end' method, I always thought. It certainly worked for Charles Agate, for when he was subsequently

established as our dropping zone officer at Tatton Park, he developed am almost unhealthy enthusiasm for jumping from the balloon.

Harry Ward

Harry Ward

Harry Ward's instructional technique may have been a bit abrupt, but there was no doubt about his own parachuting ability, as Louis Strange recalled ...
Harry Ward, that supreme artist of all parachutists, used constantly to jump with the troops, and his landings were a delight to watch. He invariably seemed to be able to control his parachute so as to fetch up alongside anyone he wished on the ground, and land like a cat, almost like a ballet dancer poised on one foot, and stepping out of his harness which he had undone just before touching ground, at the same time. Even in a high wind he seemed to be able to land on the run, and be round behind and collapsing his parachute long before it had time to be carried along the ground. I don't think I ever saw him lose his balance on landing

Louis Strange

Airborne Forces and PTS were given a major boost by the visit to Ringway in April 1941 of Winston Churchill. The demonstration of live jumping that so impressed him was probably the most important display ever given by PTS, but it was touch and go …

From 10 o'clock onwards the weather had been getting worse and at times gusted up to 25 mph, which was our limit in those days of early parachuting. Whilst our visitors were inspecting our training apparatus and listening to instructors training their squads in the hangar, the Met Office kept sending me reports of wind increasing in strength up to 35 mph. I had previously decided that the paratroops should take off whatever the weather, but that I should give Flight Lieutenant Fielden a red signal when he came over to drop them, in which case the instructors should jump and not the troops if the wind was to get much worse.

Mr Churchill was quite aware of our anxiety and asked about the wind and said we were not to take any undue risks. I assured him there would be no accident…

The troops dropped, and in fact only one strained ankle was suffered of the 40 troops landed. I had also arranged that 100 paratroopers should hide out in the long grass on the aerodrome to help the parachutists collapse their parachutes, and to join in the attack on the grandstand which had been planned. Forty parachutes in the air at one time in those early days was a wonderful sight, never seen before. Forty men running to attack a position would not be much of a show, but 140 was not so bad and I really believe that the onlookers thought they had all been landed by parachute, for we had thrown out container parachutes as well.

Louis Strange

One more quote from Louis Strange …

Sometimes the length of the stick at Tatton Park would be 600 yards when they came out too slowly. I had tried to get horses for the instructors to ride up and down the line of paratroops, giving instructions to them with megaphones, but without success.

Louis Strange

Tatton Park Balloon

Of the three balloons in use, one being called 'Bessie', decided on two occasions to untether during strong winds and fly free. One time travelling as far as Coventry before being recaptured. HW.

Tatton Park Balloon

Jumping from the balloon – introduced to Tatton Park in June 1941 – wasn't everyone's cup of tea …

Numerous stories, some apocryphal, have grown around the Tatton Park balloons. One concerns the steel handles which are screwed to the floor near where each pupil sits. Their purpose is obvious to anyone who has sat there while the car swings to and fro in the wind. But one nervous pupil is reputed to have run up to his instructor on the ground after his first descent saying, "Well, I've made it! I've jumped! But where the hell did I get these knuckle dusters from?"

Bill Jevons

Army padre sitting on the edge of the 'hole' prior to his first balloon descent: "Oh Lord, for the past 30 years I have put my faith in you. Please forgive me if for the next five seconds I transfer it to a WAAF parachute packer."

Reg McNeil

Haydn: *Of the thousands of paratroops trained at Ringway, the first two jumps were from the balloon. These jumps were generally considered most unpleasant due to the eerie silence. Especially when compared to the deafening noise and urgent slipstream of the Whitley. One paratroop Bill Watts made his first jump from the dreaded balloon in 1945. 'Wattie' had this to say after jumping from 'Bessie'.*

First Jump From the Dreaded Balloon.

We all think this Ringway's a wonderful sight
With paratroops jumping by day and by night
No more ten mile runs with rifle and pack
We've all survived Hardwick and are not going back
And Kilkenny's Circus is something to see
We sail through the air on a flying trapeze
Introduced to the Whitley, a hole in the floor
We prefer the Dakota, you jump through a door.

The balloon went up slowly to 800 feet
When it stopped with a jerk, I was white as a sheet
Then it swayed side to side as I waited my call
And I clung to the cage terrified I might fall
Then the Sergeant said "OK", it's your turn, "GO".
I jumped into space, far too proud to say "No".
As the ground rushed towards me, I looked to the sky
God! my 'chute hasn't opened, I'm going to die!

Still falling I scream, but no sound from my lips
Then the canopy opened, a crack like a whip!
A sharp tug on my harness, I hover in space
I feel I'm in heaven, a smile on my face
But an instructor below, is shouting at me
"Pull down hard on your liftwebs, you're close to a tree".
Feet and knees close together, I'm coming down fast
Forget to lean forward! Fall back on my Arse!

Bill Watts

Bill died peacefully in September 2024 just a few weeks before this book was published. I thought it might be fitting to include this into Peter's work. HW.

When Louis Strange was posted to command a trials unit for catapulting Hurricanes from the decks of merchant ships, Jack Benham took command of the Parachute Training School, but was killed on an operational sortie a few weeks later: the first PJI to give his life on active service. Maurice Newnham then took command, and in July 1941 made his first jump, from the balloon. He recalled the experience in his book 'Prelude to Glory' ...

Tatton Park Balloon

Tatton Park Balloon

I had had no preparatory training partly because I disliked physical jerks almost more than the prospect of a parachute jump and partly because Bill Hire, who gave me five minutes' verbal coaching and lent me his plimsolls, said that if I chose a calm day I should be all right.

    In deference, I suppose, to my position as newly appointed Commanding Officer of the School, the instructor in the balloon car had modified the staccato order "GO", which was normally used to dispatch pupils on their earthward journey, to a quiet and friendly intimation that all reasonable precautions had been taken to ensure that my parachute would work. "Go when you are ready," he said, and I thought cynically and desperately that I should never be ready ...

To my eternal relief, mind had gained sufficient mastery over matter to make my reluctant and personally high valued body voluntarily throw itself into space with what seemed to be a very inadequate means of support. Rock had told me that jumping from the balloon was exactly like committing suicide with a strong possibility – which you seriously doubted – that your attempt might fail. Evidently in my case the attempt hadn't failed, for there

23

was no gentle floating down to earth but a horrid violent rush which a strange feeling in my stomach assured me was no ordinary matter. Suddenly I realized that someone was shouting at me.

Tatton Park Balloon

I opened my eyes and found myself rapidly approaching the ground but with the parachute now wide open and apparently performing the function for which it was intended. "Feet together," they shouted and almost as I carried out the instruction and gripped he liftwebs firmly with my hands, I hit the ground with a bump which rattled every bone in my body.

In a moment or two I looked up to see Bill Hire grinning broadly and asking me what I thought of it. "Lovely exit," he added. "You dropped about two hundred feet before the 'chute opened – funny feeling, isn't it?"

"Words fail me," I replied.

Maurice Newnham

Haydn: *Peter Hearn's original document, did not detail Maurice Newnham's RFC pedigree as a WW1 fighter pilot with 18 victories to his credit.*

Group Captain Maurice Ashdown Newnham OBE, DFC. Originally joining the Royal Flying Corps as a 17-year-old and assigned to No.4 Squadron in France as a courier. Within 18 months he began pilot's training and posted to a Sopwith Camel unit, No. 65 Squadron. On 25 April 1918, he was shot down but three weeks later he scored his first victory by destroying an Albatros D.V. He flew 102 offensive patrols in six months, gaining more victories, including fourteen enemy fighters, a reconnaissance two-seater and three enemy observation balloons.

Newnham carried out a very successful long distance night time raid on an enemy aerodrome. Owing to heavy rain and a strong west wind he had difficulty in reaching his objective. Undeterred by this, he succeeded, and effectively bombed the aerodrome, obtaining two direct hits on a large Zeppelin shed. He then attacked other objectives, descending to ground level to do so. He returned to our lines after a 2½ hours flight. For which he received the Distinguished Flying Cross (DFC) adding an OBE to his credentials in 1944.

Group Captain Maurice Ashdown Newnham OBE, DFC (August 1897 – October 1974)

Haydn Welch

Early in his command of PTS, Maurice Newnham gained approval from the War Office for the RAF to take full responsibility for parachute training, and for PJIs henceforth to be drawn from the RAF Physical Training Branch. Which takes us into the second era of the Ringway story.

Maurice Newnham   Prelude to Glory

Maurice Newnham having received the Airborne Brevet Pegasus
from Lieutenant General F.A.M. Browning, CB.,DSO., C.O. of
Airborne Troops Royal Air Force

2 RINGWAY – THE LATER YEARS

I went on parade on 1st November, 1941, with just two balloon descents under my belt – to teach the Army how to become parachutists. The School Warrant Officer was 'Maxie' Maxwell. He had been in the Army himself before transferring to the RAF, and that was a tremendous asset. He knew what to expect from them. The night before we began, he called us all together in the crew room. "Right," he said. "Tomorrow you go out in front of the Army with the reputation that the RAF has got, of being 'Brylcreem boys', and not of being there at Dunkirk. The only way you are going to get rid of that reputation is by being better than them. One thing they are good at is drill. So tomorrow, when you go out there for the first parade, your drill is going to be immaculate. You are going to out-Guard the Guards."

Many of us had been trained as drill instructors, and we were all pretty fit and smart, so that wasn't too difficult, and it worked!

Knowing how little we really knew about the job, 'Maxie, gave us some more good advice: "If you get stuck in your synthetic training, or if someone asks you a question you can't answer, fall them into two ranks, right turn, and double march them three times round the hangar. Then bring them back and start again…" That worked as well.

Erroll Minter

Erroll recalls others amongst his contemporaries …

Guy Massey had been a ballet dancer, and anyone who thinks that ballet dancers are frail should have seen the legs on Guy! We were using the 'fan' one day, in the times before there was a device to stop the wire being wound onto the drum the wrong way – which is what happened on this day that Guy jumped with it. He came down rather swift, as you can imagine. It would have broken anyone else's leg, but Guy hit, bent his knees, said "cooorr!", straightened up, and walked away.

Billy Baker had been a Circus man – an acrobatic horse-rider with Bertram Mills. He was good value as an instructor, and as an entertainer. But there was one thing he couldn't do. He came to me after a course, when I was syndicate Flight Sergeant putting together the course reports. "Problem," he said. "What's that, Billy?" I asked. "I can't write," he said. So he told me about his section, I wrote it down, and he signed it.

Then there was Joe Sunderland, in charge of the packing section. I walked into the packing area one day, and all the girls were wearing gas-masks as they packed the 'chutes. When I asked Joe what was up, he said "Stops 'em bloody chatting: get more work done." But although he worked them hard, they loved him like a father, and nobody could get between Joe and his girls. Everyone thought the world of them.

Erroll Minter

Joe Sunderland & Harry Ward

WAAF Parachute Packers

Everyone thought the world of the ladies who ran the canteen out of Tatton Park, as well. Maurice Newnham spoke of them in his 'Prelude to Glory' ...

"Ask any pupil or instructor who trained at Ringway what he thought about the Tatton YM and he will tell you that the ladies were the kindest and the tea the nicest that he ever came across. And it was all because of Mrs Dora Smalley.

Throughout the bitter winter of 1940-1 there were no buildings or amenities of any kind at Tatton Park, and instructors and pupils had to stand about for long periods in penetrating damp or freezing wind. With the parachutists falling from the skies it was inevitable that local inhabitants should soon become aware of the general character of the work that was going on and many of them offered hospitality and assistance.

After a good deal of difficulty, for huts were scarce in those days, a Nissen was erected for the official purpose of storing equipment. In January 1942 Mrs Smalley, aided by her sister, Mrs W B Wright, Mrs Norbury and her daughter Elizabeth, opened shop under extremely uncomfortable conditions. One miserable stove, for which there was but little fuel, scarcely raised the temperature above that which prevailed outdoors but – Heaven be praised – there were cups of piping hot tea and shelter from the elements.

For four long years, tea and refreshments were served in that hut at any hour of the day or night whenever parachuting was in progress. As time went on and the number of pupils increased, it became possible to improve the facilities. The number of helpers increased too, and Phillipa Hanbury, Ann Finch-Hatton, Mrs and Rosemary Hardy and others joined the devoted band. The YM became a focal point in the School's affairs.

The senior officer or NCO regarded it as his inviolable privilege to buy the cups of tea for the whole of his stick and not infrequently the price of eleven cups – one for the instructors – was deposited before the jump, just in case.

What a weird sight the interior of that hut presented on a cold winter's evening when night jumping was in progress. A crowd of strangely garbed men, excited talking, and a dense fog of cigarette smoke. The fetid odour of sweaty – and often bloodied – humanity. Soldiers and sailors, colonels and privates, Frenchmen and Poles. RAF Sergeants basking in the homage of their admiring

29

pupils. The cheerful camaraderie, so infectious, so spontaneous – men united in a common cause and by common emotions.

Maurice Newnham

'They've Come Down To Tea'. Tatton Park, 3 June 1942

Haydn: *Having had tea and cake either before or after their balloon jumps or Whitley exits, the trainee paratroops would return to Ringway crowded onto a bus. Experiences would be shared and songs sung. This one, to the tune of John Brown's Body, perfectly summing up the black humour often encouraged by the PJIs assuming that if the men were put off jumping due to such humour, they might not be right minded to jump when the true test came.*

"Is everybody happy?" Said the Sergeant looking up.
Our hero feebly answered "Yes" and then they hooked him up.
He jumped into the slipstream and he twisted twenty times,
And he ain't gonna jump no more.

Chorus:
Glory, glory, what a hell of a way to die.
Glory, glory, what a hell of a way to die.
Glory, glory, what a hell of a way to die.
And he ain't gonna jump no more.

He counted loud, he counted long, and waited for the shock.
He felt the wind, he felt the air, he felt the awful drop.
He pulled the lines, the silk came down and wrapped around his legs. And he ain't gonna jump no more.

The days he lived and loved and laughed kept running through his mind. He thought about the medicos and wondered what they'd find. He thought about the girl back home, the one he left behind.
And he ain't gonna jump no more.

The lines all wrapped around his neck, the D rings broke his dome. The liftwebs wrapped themselves in knots around each skinny bone. The canopy became his shroud, as he hurtled to the ground.
And he ain't gonna jump no more.

The ambulance was on the spot, the jeeps were running wild.
The medicos they clapped their hands and rolled their sleeves and smiled. It had been a week or two since that a 'chute had failed.
And he ain't gonna jump no more.

He hit the ground, the sound was 'splat', the blood went spurting high. His pals were heard to say "Oh what a pretty way to die".
They rolled him up still in his 'chute, and poured him from his boots. And he ain't gonna jump no more.

There was blood upon the liftwebs, there was blood upon his 'chute. Blood that came a'trickling from the paratroopers boots.
And there he lay like jelly, in the welter of his gore.
And he ain't gonna jump no more.

Haydn Welch

An increasing number of foreign troops were trained at Ringway. Poles, Czechs, Norwegians, French, Belgians …

One officer complained that there were fourteen different nationalities represented at his lectures and his basic English was getting too involved. This is the sort of thing one heard in the hangar on the mock aperture:
"Very bad sorti. Venez back and do it encore!"
This particular Frenchmen understood – unlike the one who shouted down to the officer who was struggling bravely with the loudspeak and his French at Tatton Park:
"Spik Eenglish pliss – then I understand…"

Bill Jevons

I was in the 'medical hut' drinking tea with Doc Winfield and the Polish doctor when we saw a paratrooper lying on the ground waving a part of his parachute canopy. Doc Winfield said to the Polish doc, "He's one of yours. I recognize the landing technique." So the Pole jumped up, jumped into the jeep and drove off. We watched him as he had a few words with the injured man. He then got into the jeep, drove back, came into the hut, picked up his coffee and said "One of yours." I had difficulty in restraining a laugh as I was responsible for training the Poles in those days.

One of my pupils was a brilliant linguist in all the Scandinavian and Russian languages. His great claim to fame was that as last jumper from the aperture cage on the balloon, the cable had straightened and he actually slid down it, "With sparks flying from his boots" as reported in the Daily Mirror. He landed safely, and was eventually posted as an Intelligence Officer, but not to anywhere where his Scandinavian and Russian would be useful. I subsequently met him in Prosser's Beer Garden in Haifa where he was learning Arabic and Hebrew!

Gerry Turnbull

I found it most peculiar having to train Polish soldiers who had previously been part of the German forces. These men had been taken during action and had been inducted into the Free Polish Army in the UK.

One of my pupils had been a parachutist with the Germans and I must say that I felt very uncomfortable when standing in the door dispatching, as we did without the benefit of any restraint equipment.

There was an occasion when one of our own soldiers entered the NAFFI and recognized one of those ex-German army men as someone he had captured in hand-to-hand fighting when his own Squaddy colleague had been killed by a grenade thrown by the then-enemy. A fight ensued, whereby our Squaddy was court-martialed as being the instigator of the violence. Rough justice!

Harry Feigen

There are numerous stories about those who were reluctant to jump – or were never intended to in the first place – and were helped on their way ...

The story is told of the 'boffin' who was keen to examine the effects of a 'refusal' on the rest of the troops. He got the idea of joining a stick himself, 'refusing' to jump at a critical moment, then assessing the impact of this on the others. As he was a portly little gentleman, it was suggested that he might like to undergo some preparatory ground training. He insisted that this would not be necessary as he had no intention of actually jumping – merely 'refusing'. So the time came at six hundred feet above Tatton Park when, incognito at the head of a stick and on the flash of the green light, our little head-shrinker braced himself at the aperture and cried loudly, "I refuse to jump! I refuse to jump!"

"Like bloody 'ell you do!" muttered the dispatcher, and hurled the protesting figure bodily from the aircraft.

Harry Ward

Maurice Todhunter put a similar story into verse …
Those here referred to as One, Two, Three and Four
Were trainee paras who had jumped before.
Number five was PJI NCO –
He bellows the dreaded word "Go!".

Here at the outset it should be explained
The rules under which volunteers trained:
If during training they found aught amiss
It was back to Unit without prejudice.

Eight jumps completed – wings and elation!
Refusal then – Court Martial occasion.
Of such situation I now relate:
Refusal, and one last chance to reinstate.

The story unfolded at Tatton Park,
DZ for training in daylight and dark.
Their last chance was from the balloon, at rest –
Of all other jumps by far the safest.

Having read them the 'Fail to Obey' section
The WO added his own firm direction –
From none did he want any further sound
Until he, the last, had floated to the ground.

From the outset 'Four' pleaded with the WO
That there was something that he ought to know,
That he was not one of the Ringway batch!
That he was only there to watch!

Number One went sweating with bitten lip.
Number Two, as wished, had a push on his hip.
Number Three lunged forward, but soon lost his grip.
Then the WO turned to the Number Four drip …

The Other three feared, but had done their best.
Now the WO, riled by Four's ceaseless protest,
Firmly of his liftwebs took hold
And dropped him bodily though the hole!

Seeing the 'chute open he followed after.
Aware at once of guffaw and laughter.
When he learned of the cause from other NCOs,
Embarrassed apprehension arose

'Four' had tried to state he was no trainee,
But Services' broadsheet 'Morale' appointee.
Now fortunately happy with his new-found glory
And no longer annoyed: he had a first-hand story.

Maurice Todhunter

The Whitley was not a pleasant aeroplane to fly in, nor to jump from. "…about as awkward and uncomfortable for the job as could be imagined," said Maurice Newnham. Stan Kellaway remembers what he calls 'almost my last day at Ringway – or anywhere else' …

We had some excellent pilots at Ringway, but we had a few problems with new aircrew arrivals whose training had been much more exciting than doing circuits around Tatton Park to unload a few paratroops. Such was the occasion when Leo Brown and I were on dispatching duty with a newcomer. We were dispatching pairs – six circuits – one dummy run and five pairs to drop. I was in front of the aperture and Leo at the back, on the intercom. To cross from front to back we were supposed to lower the trap door, but no one did; after the last man had left we stepped or jumped across whilst the aircraft was still flying slow and level. I always stepped across with my left hand holding the cables that ran along the top of the fuselage. My right foot was on its way when the aircraft made a violent dive and I was thrown against the side of the fuselage. Fortunately my right hand hit the cables and I hung on, both feet through the hole. Whilst this was happening, Leo was thrown down the rear of the fuselage. Fortunately for me he wasn't hurt. He saw my predicament and crawled along the floor using ribs of the aircraft as anchor points. He grabbed my trouser leg and pulled my foot across the hole and I just got both feet on the rear edge when the aircraft did another violent movement and we both shot towards the tail. As the aircraft steadied, Leo grabbed the intercom and blasted the pilot, and he flew straight and level while we hauled in the ten bags. We didn't get a chance to see the pilot at dispersal, but I waited for him after duty. I was a Sergeant he was a Flight Lieutenant, but he got my meaning. He apologized, but admitted that he completely forgot that there were still two of us aboard after the troops had gone. He had been a fighter pilot…

Stan Kellaway

Whitley Exit

Other recollections of the Whitley …

Engine fumes and the reek of vomit tested the strongest stomach, and dispatchers bent double by the low fuselage, pulling in strops and bags, were hard put to do so in the few minutes before landing at Ringway. Officially that duty lay with the dispatchers forward and aft of the aperture, for each to haul in five strops, since the trainees sat fore and aft in sardine fashion prior to "swivel legs, sit, heave and drop." Ironically a notice on the half-circular aperture doors forbade crossing the aperture without first closing the doors – an almost impossible edict in view of streamed strops.

Sergeant Paul and I were teamed up with Maxie Schonback, a brilliant but extrovert South African pilot. We were routinely hauling in the strops when an unexpected steep power dive sent both of us sprawling, dragged by the strops to the aperture and powerless to brace against the side. Just as suddenly, head over aperture, we were glued there, as we pulled out of the dive at full power, and we scrabbled backward as the plane leveled out.

It was typical of Maxie: he had spotted his wife and children at the swimming pool and had the impulse to dive-bomb them. His reply to our shaky protestations was also typical: we hadn't fallen out and in any case we were wearing parachutes.

Maurice Todhunter

Stationed at Aircrew Wing - Yatesbury, Ron Williams and myself were posted to Ringway in July 1943 to take the initial 8-descent Army Course, returning to Yatesbury to teach aircrew trainees parachute ground training, before going back to Ringway in 1944 as staff instructor.

Alan Pope was my instructor. Having done two balloon descents I felt confident. My next descent was 'pairs' from a Whitley, which went off okay. The next descent – stick of five from the Whitley – was when it happened. Shuffling along the aircraft on my bottom with my knees tucked under my chin I swung my feet into the 'hole' and pushed off with my hands to make my exit. I was facing the engines and remember the slipstream hitting me and tilting me forward.

On landing, I rolled my 'chute and started to make my way to the tea hut for a cup of char and a wad, when one of the lads mentioned that my chin and neck were covered in blood, "You've rung the bell !" they all cheered.

I hadn't felt a thing. I went to the medical hut at Tatton Park where Doc Winfield put a few stitches in my chin. Making my exit I had hit it on the aperture, which prevented me from doing a somersault.

Walking about the Station with my chin plastered up meant that I was forever being ridiculed - all in good fun, of course. Being a Corporal at the time, I was spared the custom of drinks-all-round in the Sergeants Mess.

Jimmy Blythe
(Sergeant, not Gp Capt)

Jumping Through The 'Hole'.

And then there were the water descents…

At ten o'clock on the morning of Christmas Day, half a dozen of us performed the Ringway Ceremony, which I had inaugurated the year before, known as "The Mortification of the Flesh". The ritual was quite simple – we parachuted from 700 feet into the deep waters of Rostherne Mere. This was regarded by a very few as a suitable prelude to the day's festivities. I noticed, however, that of the previous year's enthusiasts only one, Joe Sunderland, felt the necessity for being mortified with me a second time. As the temperature was forty degrees Fahrenheit and the wind stung like a whip, the decision was perhaps not altogether surprising.

Maurice Newnham

During a long spell of bad weather we tried several times to drop an important Marine officer into water. He was a specialist in limpet mines. At last the day came for his descent and the DZ Party were well briefed for action with the rescue boat. They had to get as close as they could to where he landed; this man was too important to drown. They did their job too well: he landed slap in the middle of the boat on the engine cover, and broke his leg.

Stan Kellaway

Random reminiscences from Ringway

Sergeant Billy Baker (the Bertram Mills circus rider) once dispatched a stick of ten Polish Paratroops over the Cheshire countryside between Ringway and Tatton Park instead of over the DZ. The CO received a telephone message from the Knutsford police to say that a local farmer had rounded up what he thought were ten German paratroops. Transport was dispatched and the driver found the Poles cowering in the corner of a barn with a burly farmer guarding them with a pitchfork.

When Billy appeared before the CO he described what had happened. "Suddenly the red light came on, then the green, and before I could say anything, there they were – gone!"

It was decided that the mistake was caused by a freak shaft of bright Spring sunshine which had caught the red light, then moved to the green.

Reg McNeil

We had this 'Scouse' trainee. When he jumped from the aircraft, his 'chute didn't open. Roman Candle – waving about like a candle flame above his head. He hit the ground and bounced and the parachute descended over him like a shroud. We instructors didn't bother to run to him because we knew he would be dead. However, the parachute suddenly moved. We went over and pulled off his shroud, and this white-faced, 6-foot Liverpudlian sat up and said "I didn't do a very good landing, did I Sarge…"

"Lie down, Scouse. You should be dead," we told him. He was in hospital for nigh on six months, but he lived to tell the tale.

Peter Tingle

Nearly fifty ex-schoolmasters were to become parachute instructors. One visiting General, while informally inspecting a parade of instructors, made conversation by asking each man what his job was before the war. After getting the same answer ten times in succession, he was heard to mutter, "Not another bloody schoolmaster!"

Bill Jevons

There was the instructor who, dispatching from a Whitley, after several sorties and bursting for a pee, relieved himself through the aperture whilst airborne. On landing, he discovered that No 1 in the stick, who had watched the performance with interest, was a female of 'E' syndicate – the Specials – who had been indistinguishable from the others in her smock and rubber helmet.

Val Valentine

Someone decided that a news film should be made to show the British Public our wonderful Parachute Troops. So a film unit arrived. They had to make best use of the limited material available. In one sequence the troops were marching in threes out of a hangar and as they passed the camera they doubled back, reformed and marched out again, and again, and again. Very impressive, it looked. I was attached to a cameraman who we mounted on a trolley and I pushed him backwards and forwards for close up and long shots: the early version of the tele-photo lens. For the aircraft descents we used three Whitleys many times and the shots were edited to give the impression of a mass drop...

Stan Kellaway

Billy Baker, a first class tumbler, was in our gymnastic display team, but never attended practice. During a display at Hardwick he went for a round-off back somersault. Being out of practice he pulled his Achilles tendon. So for a time he was swinging along on crutches and working in the detail-office, which was a nice little number. He used to catch the 5 o'clock bus to a regular appointment, and on one occasion his watch was slow and as he went for the bus it started to move away. He put both crutches under one arm and executed a sprint worthy of an international athlete.

John Savill

The shortest instructor was Wee Robbie Robertson, an ex-circus acrobat (the top man on the pyramid). He had been dispatching from a Whitley and when the aircraft stopped taxiing, Robbie took a short cut and dropped through the hole in the floor. Unfortunately, the aircraft hadn't reached the tarmac. It was still on the peri-track, and as Robbie's feet touched the ground the aircraft moved forward. He was too short to climb back and he dare not fall to the ground because of the tail wheel, so he ran and kept on running until the aircraft came to a final halt. You can image the sight of an aircraft with a pair of legs running beneath the fuselage.

Stan Kellaway

Just before the School moved to Upper Heyford, Warrant Officer Jack Roy called for those "not allocated to classes" - which meant most of us re-mustered ex-aircrew types - and explained that as there were some personnel from Allied Parachute Schools being shown over No 1 PTS, we should go round the training area and make sure that all was clean and tidy. This was how I found myself at the vast mat section with two fourteen-foot trestle steps, with cables from the roof of the hangar down to a wooden handgrip near the ground.

I was busy sorting out the mats when Squadron Leader Jimmy Blyth came into view with a crowd of Officers in various foreign uniforms covered with medal ribbons and gold braid. To my horror they assembled all around the mats and Jimmy called upon me to demonstrate "this piece of equipment".

In true PTS fashion I grasped the hand piece and sped off to the nearest trestle. Halfway up I started to turn, when a voice said "Go to the top, will you." Nobody ever went from there!

I thought "Bloody Nora", and wobbled my way onto the top. Having arrived, I found it very difficult to hold the handle and turnabout in order to do the exercise. My head being some twenty feet from the ground, and perched on a very small and unsteady platform, at the sight of the mats in the distance I almost fainted. However, I grasped the hand-piece firmly, jumped upwards and backwards to take the strain on the cable, and hurtled to the ground. On impact it seemed that many nasty things happened to me simultaneously. This tinged with an attack of pandemonium summed up the situation, but I was determined not to let the side down, so I hung on, and through the dense cloud of dust and stuff that I had created, what was left of me completed the 'roll'. Feet together, knees together, elbows in and chin on chest.

With my very best sickly grin, I pushed myself up onto one elbow to look at the Chief Instructor, and to my mortification found that the entire party had moved on to the next apparatus. I fell back onto the mat and started to check over the damage when a voice said "Get up man for God's sake! You're making the place look untidy." I had just gone full circle. It was WO Jack Roy.

Nolan May

"Say Sarge, suppose I jump out and the 'chute doesn't open? What then?"

"I'd say you were jumping to a conclusion …"

Anon

In 'Prelude to Glory', Maurice Newnham tells of the great buildup of our Airborne Forces towards its eventual strength of two Divisions …

Throughout the summer, autumn and winter of 1943 and the spring of 1944 the great hangar-gymnasium echoed and re-echoed with the incessant clatter of the training apparatus, the commands of the instructors and the thuds of the pupils' tumbling bodies. At Tatton Park men jumped from balloons and aircraft by day and night, weekdays and Sundays, whenever weather conditions were suitable. Six – seven – eight hundred – a thousand men at a time were housed and trained at Ringway in preparation for the tremendous events which were drawing near.

The RAF Station throbbed with the movement of marching men – men going briskly and cheerfully from one type of instruction to another … Men of many nations, nice men, brave men – all learning to inflict greater hurt upon the enemy.

Life for those instructors, and the whole School, was hectic indeed during those busy, exciting months.

Maurice Newnham

These 'tremendous events' to which Maurice Newnham referred were the great airborne operations in Europe – the drops into Normandy, at Arnhem, and across the Rhine. Before then – since the earliest days, in fact – PJIs had been acting as operational dispatchers for SAS troops and 'Specials'. One of them was John Savill …

In November 44 I was sent to the 2nd SAS. Duties included parachute training and dispatching SOE, Special Allied Army Recce Force, as well as SAS. On one occasion I went with a party of eleven SAS who were training for an operation in Norway to drop them and their skis on an exercise in France, near Grenoble. The DZ was on a slope, and as we ran in with the first stick of six at action stations, the ground came closer and closer until the shadow of the Stirling on the snow completely blotted out the aperture which was like a huge bath. I didn't receive any instructions but put the troops into crash positions, and sure enough there was an almighty thump from the tail end. The strop bar which projected below the tail wheel had struck the very top of the mountain. I climbed along the side of the aperture and managed to clear it from the control wires – for which the captain was grateful – and fix it for another run. We got the first stick out this time, and on the next run I put the bundles of skis out. They were longer than the aperture, and one bundle got stuck, with the 'chute deployed in the slipstream. I tried jumping on them. Someone handed me a fighting knife. That did the trick. By the time I got the other five men away, there was a right mess of tangled strops, bags and rigging lines, and getting it all in was no small problem.

When the SAS team got back from France, I eventually went with them to launch the operation from a Scottish base. We were isolated from the rest of the Station. The weather was bad and the operation was postponed daily, until it was eventually cancelled. The SAS weren't going to let all that good explosive go to waste though. I was sitting in the NAFFI when there was an almighty explosion. One of the handles of the metal dustbin sailed through the window of the dental surgery and finished up on the instrument tray. The Station Admin Officer was not amused.

John Savill

Short Stirling

Sergeant Phil Wilding and Pilot officer Frank Copland lost their lives on these 'Special' missions, and Leo Brown came pretty close to it, as he narrated to Maurice Newnham …

We took off from Fairford in a Stirling with eight French parachutists, their kitbags, and a load of twelve containers. Between Alderney and Cap de la Hague we were hit by AA fire and one of the men was injured. The aircraft was damaged by holes in the fuselage and petrol tanks … Shortly afterwards the pilot told me to prepare for ditching as the aircraft was losing height and becoming increasingly difficult to handle. The altimeter was broken and the darkness made it impossible to estimate the height or how long it would take before we hit the sea.

I ordered the troops to take ditching positions. There was some panic and I had to help most of the men remove their parachutes … I gave the warning, "Brace for impact," and the aircraft hit the sea with a terrific shock. There was an immediate inrush of water into the cockpit and fuselage. The kitbags, which were lying aft of me, shot forward and I was carried into the wireless operator's compartment. I struggled to get into the fuselage … The Flight Engineer and I managed to carry the wounded man over the main spar, through the fuselage, up the ladder and laid him on top of the fuselage which was above water level.

I checked up on the men and found that two were missing, so I went back to find them. One was standing in the fuselage shouting "Je ne sais pas nager" and I saw that he had not inflated his lifebelt. I managed to get him to the ladder and pushed him out onto the top fuselage. The second man was lying between two kitbags and I saw that he was dead…

We put the injured man and the air gunner on the bottom of the dinghy and the rest of the crew and parachutists sat around the side, the pilot and I then commenced to swim, pushing the dinghy in front of us. We had moved about a hundred yards when the aircraft sank – she had stayed afloat for twelve minutes. After a few more minutes I found that I could no longer carry on, owing to pain in my back and left leg. A little later the Captain also had to give up. The remainder of the crew and troops were in no fit condition to swim as most of them had either been wounded or injured in the crash. The pilot decided to throw out the sea-anchor and wait to see whether the radio's SOS had been picked up. The sea was calm, but bailing out had to be done with a field-service cap which was the only article available. In about twenty minutes we saw the lights of a vessel ... the wireless operator flashed a signal with a torch. In about half an hour an Air Sea Rescue launch came alongside the dinghy and took us into Cherbourg Harbour.

Leo Brown

When Paris was liberated, fifteen Crois de Guerre were awarded to the SAS for their valiant assistance to the Resistance forces within France. The SAS promptly passed four of the medals to PTS instructors – one of them going to Leo Brown.

Before then, the 6th Airborne Division had jumped into Normandy to spearhead the D-Day invasion. Who should be in the lead-aircraft, but Louis Strange, now Wg Cdr Air Ops with 46 Group!

At 2315 hours on June 5th, 1944, Squadron Leader Dusty Miller, the pilot of the first aircraft of the leading Squadron of 46 Group, in which I was Acting as Group observer, assistant dispatcher, general cabin-boy and steward to the paratroops, eased off the brakes and eased the throttle forward. The aircraft rolled forward, taxiing and turning to the end of the runway, gathered speed, and took off into the west, where the last red glow of the sunset lingered.

In two thousand aircraft and gliders the airborne troops were singing. In our aircraft, having gone right through "Tipperary", they settled down to verse after verse of a song in which they found a lovely aircraft but couldn't find the lovely DZ, and when they found the lovely DZ they couldn't find the lovely pub, and when they found the lovely pub they couldn't find the lovely barmaid. When they found the lovely barmaid she couldn't find the lovely beer, and the chorus from time to time let it be known that they were very much obliged to some almighty power which directed that everything should happen to their complete discomfiture. Verse after verse, until one by one they settled down and dropped quietly off to sleep, having been about three quarters of an hour airborne.

The night was clear, and there was still just enough light to see the streams of Dakotas in arrowhead threes. The first thing I noticed as we got well out over the Channel was what at first appeared to be a rough sea, with many white horses ahead. On passing over and looking carefully down, I saw that these were the bow waves of hundreds of sea-going craft, all in perfect order and formation. I think that moment gave us the greatest thrill of all so far. The hunt was up, the invasion on. We of airborne forces had started scratch, but we were now overhauling the main body of the hunt: we were to lead the vanguard in to the kill.

While still a long way off the coast, we saw the great flashes and explosions of the 100 – Lancaster bombing raid on the armoured battery of coastal defence guns, situated almost on our track at the little village of Merville. This tough nut was to be cracked wide open by the 9th Battalion of the Parachute Regiment and three gliders manned by troops whose stern duty it was to land, not near, but ON the battery.

It was with great difficulty that we allowed the paratroops to sleep on peacefully with the coastline looming up ahead, but there was no purpose in getting them ready too soon. The signal for Action Stations was given ten minutes before the time for dropping. Immediately all was bustle and activity, parachutes and kit-bags adjusted and checked, static lines freed and hooked up, each man checking his neighbour's safety catch and pin. The wireless operator and I took up positions at the rear of the cabin, just behind the exit door, ready for the dispatch. The pilot was steadily throttling back his engine to lose height down to 500 feet, and the coastline became clear cut, little white crests of waves breaking on the beach. As we passed over the coastline we let go our anti-personnel bombs, to keep the German's heads down and to make them think we were bombers.

We were half way from the coast to the DZ before I noticed much anti-aircraft fire, and then it was too high and well behind us. A certain amount of red tracer flew up in bursts around and about, but by and large the AA defences were nothing like as bad as we had expected. The lights of the pathfinders were showing plainly ahead of us as the red 4-second warning light came on: the longest four seconds in a man's life. The engines are throttled further back, the nose of the aircraft rises slightly, the slope of the floor is towards the rear now. The leader of the stick is silhouetted in the doorway, arms outstretched at shoulder height, gripping the sides, ready to spring. The remainder are crowding and closing up behind him, like a queue of strap-hangers waiting to get out of a tube train at rush hour. The red light changes to green, a bell rings loudly above the muffled engines. Instantly, but only as an aid, and as a reassuring confirmation, the dispatcher's hand slaps down hard on Number One's shoulder, he disappears, is gone, another silhouette immediately fills the gap and is gone ... like flickering black shadows they go, pouring out almost touching each other, like a pack of cards falling. What a sight! What a moment! Those sixteen paratroopers were out in eight seconds. Two more sticks of sixteen were going down from our numbers 2 and 3, and from the stream of aircraft behind, 48 troops every fifteen seconds would be backing them up. The gallant 6th Airborne were pouring, teeming down the night sky into action in the vanguard of the most remarkable invasions. For a moment the aircraft felt very lonely and empty: the urge to follow those splendid troops was almost irresistible.

Louis Strange

Amongst the PJIs who dispatched troops onto the drop zones of Arnhem was George Podevin ...

As a Flight Lieutenant, I was attached to Brigadier John Hackett's 4th Parachute Brigade HQ in August 1944. The purpose was to assist with the air training and dispatching prior to 1st Airborne Div's participation in the British and American advance in Europe. There were many other officers and NCO PJIs scattered throughout the division employed in this way. There were four large Exercises in preparation for the real thing. I dispatched the troops on Exercises 'Stop Gap' and 'Bloater', and parachuted as the last man on 'Alace' and 'Dice'. On Exercise 'Dice', the Brigade Padre was jumping just in front of me. When 13 got to the door, he hesitated, thus delaying the stick, so that by the time the Padre and I got to the door we were already running out of DZ. We eventually landed close together and quite heavily in the edge of a corn field. After getting out of our harnesses, we decided to sit down and get our breath back before trying to locate the main body. It was then that the Padre reached into his jumping jacket and pulled out a bottle of wine at the same time saying, "Our need, oh my comrade, is greater than theirs." And so we sat there drinking the wine that should have been used at that next communion service.

There were many postponements of the operation proper. Finally, however, it was decided that the 1st Airborne Division, along with the Polish Brigade, should drop at Arnhem and capture the bridge there. The rest, of course, is well known history.

I went over to Arnhem as Dispatcher, firstly with the advance HQ Group of 4th Para Brigade on 17th September, then on the following day with the main body of the Brigade. On both occasions we were subjected to a certain amount of light flack and small-arms fire, but no damage done.

The PJIs, their duty completed, returned to Ringway. I decided to stay and offer my services to the Poles, but due to bad visibility they were not able to drop on the following day as planned. In fact, they were held up by bad weather for the next three days and eventually took off from Saltby on 21st September. In the meantime, the Germans knew that they were yet to come and were therefore well prepared to receive them. The Poles really had a rough time. We had no opposition until we reached the DZ near Elden. It was then that we had a great deal of flak from anti-aircraft small-arms fire. The enemy shot at the aircraft, at the troops when they were airborne, and when they landed. I saw two of the aircraft on my port side catch fire while the troops were still jumping out. The planes eventually crashed.

The American Quartermaster of my aircraft, as soon as the last man had been dispatched, cut all the trailing static lines away in order to reduce drag. We then dived down to 1900 feet to gather speed to avoid the flack and turned to starboard to clear the DZ, which by that time was a very unpleasant place to be.

The pilot proceeded to make his was back to his UK base, but was handicapped by persistent fog. After some hours of flying we eventually arrived over the English coast. By this time the aircraft was running out of fuel. The pilot was now making large circuits over the coast and out to sea again, the fog still persisting. At last he made a decision and in a loud voice declared, "Well, I guess Uncle Sam's had this ****** aircraft: I'm gonna ditch." At this I thought to myself, on the basis of the devil I knew, I would prefer to parachute out and take my chances. I said as much to the pilot whose response was "Okay, if that's the way you want it." Fortunately for us all, however, while I was fitting my parachute, a search-light battery, aware of our plight, shone a beam into the sky, indicating that we were over land and near an airfield.

The pilot made a safe landing eventually, declaring that we were at Plymouth. We were in fact, at Manston airfield in Kent. 138 miles off course from base, and 250 miles from Plymouth.

George Podevin

One of the PJI despatchers on the last great airborne assaults – the crossing of the Rhine – was Norman Goodacre. It had long been Norman's ambition to jump with his troops on a real operation, and although he didn't put it in his report, he never had any intention of flying back across the Rhine once the aircraft had crossed it ...

I was dispatcher on Dakota chalk 67, taking off at 1715 hours on 24th March 1945, flying in formation, and the crew were of the American 9th AF.

At 0954, on crossing the River Rhine, anti-aircraft fire was directed at the formation. I saw Chalk 68 was hit on fire and Chalk 69 was also flying with difficulty. A few moments later my aircraft was thrown violently over on its side, throwing the stick of men on the floor. I am not certain whether this was a hit from flack or evasive action from another aircraft in difficulty. The crew chief came from the cabin, adjusting his flack suit, and shouted "All out."

By this time the men were regaining order, the Green light was on, and I started to dispatch them. Flack was fairly thick by now, and the machine-gun fire was coming from the enemy on the DZ. The crew chief again called "All out" and re-entered the cabin. The aircraft was very unsteady, and having no time, I took his order to represent the English equivalent of "Abandon aircraft".

Since we had been previously briefed that dropping height was 450 feet, I was wearing an 'X' type, and was hooked up on No 1 strop. I jumped, and landed some 200 yards from the stick on the DZ. This was held by the enemy, so having no choice, I went into action with the stick.

After two days with the stick, I made contact with the OC Glider Regiment at Bislich, Upper Wesel, and was attached to them until such times that an aircraft was available to return us to England, where I arrived on the 31st March.

Norman Goodacre

When the final battle was won, Lieutenant General Richard Gale, General Officer Commanding 1st British Airborne Corps, wrote the following tribute to the Parachute Training School:

To all who qualified and subsequently fought as parachutists, the happiest memories are associated with this great School. Here no less than four hundred thousand live descents by parachute were made during the war and no less than sixty thousand British and Allied parachutists were trained. The spirit that has animated so many of them to perform such grand and courageous tasks was largely laid at the Parachute Training School.

Richard Gale

Lieutenant General Richard Gale

3 MIDDLE EAST PTS

PTS Missionaries have travelled far and wide preaching the gospel of safe parachuting. The first Chief Instructor at the India Parachute School was Squadron Leader Brereton, who came to Ringway when PTS was born. When the story of the Burma front is written, there will be many references to the help given by PTS to the 14th Army and the Chindits. Another party of instructors went out to train paratroops in Egypt and Palestine, and they have made many perilous trips over the mountains into Yugoslavia.

Bill Jevons

THE MIDDLE EAST

When David Stirling started training his own SAS parachutists in the Middle East, the initial results were disastrous. Four PJIs from Ringway were eventually sent out to help: Jim 'Ginger' Averis, Ian 'Mac' McGregor, 'Natch' Markwell, and Ken 'Joe' Welch – who went three good rounds with Bruce Woodcock on the 'Windsor Castle' on the way out. These four became known as 'The Middle East Toffs' ... The Four Toffs received that illustrious title from the SAS after the realization that together they had a reputation for doing rather well with cards.

Friendly relationships were soon established with the mess members of the SAS under CSM Riley, and we were soon joined by half a dozen Army parachuting instructors under Sergeant Major Johnny Dawes and all worked together as a team.

Two high ranking Yugoslav officers and a Serbian Sergeant were our first trainees and were soon away to join General Mihailovitch. It was about this time that 'Ginger' Averis went as dispatcher with an agent to some destination 'beyond the Danube'. The 'plane was a Liberator whose large interior was almost filled with supplementary fuel tanks. It took off from Fayed at 6pm and landed back fourteen and a half hours later. Other trips but not quite of that duration followed. Memories will vary. One of the strongest may be the frustration and anti-climax of having to return when the DZ could not be identified. Others may remember the preliminary preparations when one could be asked to count out hundreds of gold sovereigns for insertion into body-belts. Perhaps the most poignant memory was to see fires burst into life as the noise of the aircraft was picked up below – enemy decoys, or desperate pleas for help? One could never tell, and the pilot could only fly on in search of pre-arranged signals.

In the early autumn of '42, three of us were sent to Heliopolis and took part in an odd adventure that caused not a little apprehension. Some obscure branch of the Service decided that with the Germans at Alamein it might be useful to threaten the largely Italian-held garrison at the oasis of Siwa by dropping parachutists followed by a pyrotechnic display. In consequence three Hudson aircraft were loaded with dummy parachutists each filled with cordite, much of which was stowed by the instructors, and each dummy having a pull-type detonator. Ten men and a despatcher were always a rather tight fit in the Hudson and egress through the side door always called for a certain shrinking-type movement. Dispatching ten uncooperative dummies each liable to go up in flames if primed too early was not particularly amusing. In the event after a flight of a little over two hours all dummies were dispatched safely.

By early '43 we lost the Army instructors with some sadness; they were able, congenial colleagues and it was generally regretted that they could not apparently be transferred to the RAF. Several of them distinguished themselves with SOE in the Balkans. No mention of the early days on the Middle East School would be complete without reference to one of the early overseas recruits to the staff, one Jimmy Seddon, largely known as 'Hab Dab', 'The Mighty One', or even 'Nod-em-in Seddon' – the last title due to his claimed prowess on the soccer field. He was a natural comedian with a fund of good stories and an ability to recite Lancashire monologues with all the conviction of Stanley Holloway.

With the allied armies driving the enemy from North Africa, the Middle East Parachute School moved to Ramat David aerodrome about twenty miles from Haifa.

Jim Averis

Consolidated B-24 Liberator

Another of 'The Middle East Toffs' recalls ...

In late October 1942 I was amazed and delighted to find myself chosen to train two New Zealanders (Capt Scott who was later recommended for the VC for his part in the destruction of the viaduct at Thermoplae, and Sgt Bob Morton) to make a decent directly behind the German lines at Alamein. Following intensive training I supervised the distribution of their equipment about their persons. This included climbing irons for shinning up telegraph poles – not the nicest things to sit down on – and water bottles handy on the chests, and rations for a few days lay-up.

We loaded up (the Wellington) and our first port of call from Kabrit was to a desert outpost and a visit to the legendary – even at that time – Captain David Stirling, for briefing.

We were to fly out at about 8pm in bright moonlight, and two hours before the battle of Alamein started we were to run in from the Mediterranean onto the coast on El Alamein about a quarter-mile behind the German front line, at less than 1000 feet, to a point a few miles south, where according to the latest aerial photographs there was no build-up of troops. Here the New Zealanders would hop out at 350 feet and proceed to cut all telegraphic communications between south and north. They would then hole up and wait for the armour to roll back, let the British line move over them – David Stirling said the troops would be too trigger happy for introductions at that time – and then report to somebody responsible. It sounded a bit dicey.

Now that I knew battle was about to commence, I eagerly looked out as we flew forward for what I was sure would be wave after wave of tanks in every direction, but all I saw was a M25-style processing along the coast road.

Come 19.30 and we were all ready, everything checked, and away we went out to sea, then back to the coast and overland. Then it all started. In my opinion we were fired at from both Germans and British, and for a long time I remembered the repeated song of the 'pom-poms'. A plaintive note from the rear gunner "They're hose-piping at us Captain, can you jig it about a bit?" Then a classic comment from the front gunner, who when asked by the Captain what he could see, said "Bugger all 'till I open my bleeding eyes, Guv." Then our gunners retaliated and the Wellington filled with cordite smoke, and the Captain calmly began his countdown, "Ten … nine … eight …" whilst I got the New Zealanders over the hole. Then to my horror I could see men running about on the ground 300-400 feet below, with upturned faces and flashing guns.

At that moment the port side was hit amidships by a cannon shell, taking the canvas off a large area and damaging the geodetics. One glance at No 1 over the hole was enough to advise Captain to abort. No 1 had faced the blast, his face was a mass of blood and as I pulled him back from the hole, I could see his upper lip was cut away and the front of his body was wet through. "What's wrong with my mush, Mark?" he said.

I patched him up while we shot off down to Siwa to a hospital base. The lower half of his body was wet through because a large piece of shrapnel had penetrated the front wall of his water bottle, but had not got through to his chest. Without that water bottle he would have been killed.

We were de-briefed, and delayed-action bombs were later dropped along the route of the telegraph lines. For my part, I went for a short rest whilst a surgeon removed some shrapnel from one eye, and I accepted with great pleasure the bottles of Guinness that my colleagues smuggled in for me.

'Natch' Markwell

('Natch' – so called because of his fortunate habit of rolling a seven or eleven in a crap game.)

Vickers Wellington

Gerry Turnbull became involved in operations of a different sort whilst at Ramat David ...

One of the most gallant girls I trained was a Polish girl called Christine (at least that was the best we could do with her name, which contained a couple of Xs, Ys and Zs). I used to fly with her and dispatch her, and usually on her return she would ring and we would meet for dinner. On one occasion she rang and said she was in the Officers Club and for security reasons couldn't come out, but could I come over and have a meal there. A slight problem: I was a Warrant Officer at the time!

However, using our Middle East ingenuity as detailed in the training film shown at PTS, I approached my CO, one Spud Murphy, and explained the problem. Instant solution: he handed me his rank badges and said "Off you go and don't get caught."

Everything went fine. We had a splendid meal and life was very pleasant until a bottle of champagne was brought to the table by a waiter, with a handwritten note. The note said, "Congratulations! Come and see me in the morning", signed by a very senior officer.

Luckily he was an Aussie who knew me well. He handed me the biggest rocket I'd had for a while, then said "Who was the girl?" I explained, and he said "Come back at 14:00."

I went back expecting almost anything. He gave me another rocket and then said, "I've rung your CO and given him a bad time and we have mutually decided to send you back to the UK." This was a terrible shock, but as I saluted and turned about to go, he added a throw-away postscript, "You will be on the next commissioning course at Cosford…"

What happened to the girl? She survived six drops into occupied territory before she left her job as an agent. Unable to settle, she took a job on a trans-Atlantic liner and made legal history by being murdered and her body disposed of by being pushed through a porthole. The steward was arrested, tried, and convicted of murder. First case in legal history with such a verdict being brought in without a body.

Gerry Turnbull

We must accept some of these anecdotes as being, well, maybe just stories. The case of The Porthole Murder involved a steward working on the Durban Castle, convicted to hang in 1947. He appealed at around the same time moves were being made to end capital punishment. He escaped his date with the hangman and his sentence reduced to life. Churchill was apparently furious. The lady in question had served in the Auxiliary Territorial Service (ATS) and may (or not) be the lady remembered by Gerry. She being an English actress Eileen Gibson (known as Gay) was born in 1926. The steward, James Camb was a womaniser, although it seems Gay might also have been accustomed to brief encounters. (I hope Gerry remained a true gentlemen). Whatever happened that night in 1947, the steward protested his innocence to murder, stating Gay (sailing as a first class passenger) died during a night of passion. In his haste, he pushed her body through the porthole into the shark infested ocean around West Africa. Camb was released from prison after eleven years but went on to make further attacks and returned to prison to complete the full sentence.

Haydn Welch

Gay Gibson

Harry Feigen remembers another lady, called Sally ...

One of our Sergeants who shall be nameless, persuaded one of the late King Farouk's pets (a dachshund dog) to leave the Palace grounds in Cairo, whereby she was kidnapped and became the well-loved camp pet of Ramat David. Sally, as she was named, became an ace parachutist after some ground training. She became excited when her minder was about to emplane, and in her own canine way showed a desire to emulate his jump activities – which she did with the usual nervous reaction that her human counterparts invariably show. With a specifically designed parachute, she did her full complement of jumps, with a few plus.

When shipped back to the UK and put into quarantine, she unfortunately pined for her master. Despite regular visits, she passed away. It was believed of a broken heart. Aaaaaahhh ...

Harry Feigen

Jim Averis tells the story of George Howard who – following the practice of releasing the 'box', easing out of the harness, and hanging by the hands prior to landing – let go at about 100 feet, pitched into fortunately damp ground flat on his face, to leave a remarkable likeness imprinted in the soil, then get up and walk away. '

(The following account is taken from a memoir written by Jim in 1991 and supplied to Haydn in 2024 just before the publication of this volume. The details were missed out of Peter's original collection but well worth adding now.

A practice favoured by the more experienced instructors, not officially approved but doubtless practiced at all Schools, enabled the performer to release his box at a hundred feet or so above the ground, ease out of the leg straps and then suspended by the arms, glide to make a stand-up landing with the parachute relieved of the jumper's weight and drifting to earth near one's feet. No doubt a stupid, needless risk but an accomplishment very satisfying to the performer!

Alas for unfortunate imitators, things are not always quite as easy as they seem. It was a splendid morning when George made the first descent of the day; a good exit and uneventful flight until around one hundred feet above the ground, George and the parachute parted company. The parachute, now lightened, lost its elegant rotundity and drifted slowly yet gracefully towards the earth. All eyes of course were on George, and what were surely his last moments on this earth. With a seemingly relaxed position, yet almost as if he were holding himself at attention in order to make a tidy exit from this world, he fell earthwards; slightly pivoting forwards as he fell, he eventually hit the ground in a perfectly horizontal position.

George, it should be mentioned here, had been a very successful boxer and in, it is thought, the middle weight class. As we raced the thirty yards or so, considering what words might be appropriate to comfort the dying if in fact he was not already dead, we were amazed to see movement from the 'body'. "Lie still !" we yelled, but to no avail, for by the time we reached him, George was on his feet – distinctly shaking but with that "I've beaten the count of ten" look.

The truly memorable part of the affair was the impression left in the Dropping Zone by George's body. The area had been a maize field and there was an imprint five or six inches deep, that filled with plaster would have provided a superb model for Madam Tussauds. Every item of his clothing was clearly discernable in the finest detail – boot eyelets and laces, every ridge in the twill of his jumping suit, the stubble-marked chin that clearly demonstrated that he had not shaved, lined forehead and bushy eyebrows were all clearly displayed. Perhaps the most dramatic of all, two neatly curved piles of earth that had been forced up his nostrils.

Amazingly George appeared to suffer no adverse after-effects; he was urged to take things quietly for the rest of the day.

Jim Averis

'Natch' Markwell provided the sequel ...

We trained a Gurkha troop about the same time. They had seen us divest ourselves of our harness and hang on the liftwebs, and maybe they even saw George fall. Certainly on their first jump we were horrified to see them all releasing themselves in the air and falling out all over the place. Further dropping was temporarily suspended, but none of those tough little men suffered any injury.

'Natch' Markwell

Also not included in the original collection from Peter. Jim reported this far more serious matter.

It was shortly after George's jump that there occurred a most remarkable parachuting accident. The incident could be summarized as a single exit but three landings. The tragedy began with the parachute descent of the morning programme.

A trainee parachutist made a normal exit followed by a typical descent with a landing a few feet from the officer on duty. The landing was for a trainee most unusually, in that feet together he made an effortless standing landing. As the soldier prepared to operate his box, the parachute, which had remained full and stationary above his head, slowly lifted the parachutist to fifty feet or sixty feet before slowly returning him to the ground, and for a second stand-up landing that was almost a replica of the first.

Again the trainee moved to undo his box but once again he was lifted into the sky – but this time much more violently, and was swept a hundred or so feet across and away from the dropping zone before descending in vicious spirals a hundred or more yards beyond the boundary where, with amazing ill fortune, he was smashed into the side of a solitary farm wagon. He died almost immediately.

Jim Averis

Alf Card, who joined the Middle East School in 1942 and moved with it to Ramat David, remembers one of the original 'Four Toffs' – 'Joe' Welch…

On June 1st, 1943, I was dispatching my trainees on the final descent. I was loading them aboard when 'Joe' came up with his lop-sided grin and said that he was making a descent after my stick had been dropped. I then noticed that his 'chute was not your usual run-of-the-mill static line job'. For a start there was a ripcord, and he was also wearing a reserve. "What's that, Joe?" I asked.

"A trainer main," was the reply. The pilot a Canadian called Tommy Read who apparently knew all about it as he didn't turn a hair when I told him Joe was aboard and wanted to be dropped from 2000 feet. Later I found out from Joe that he had come across the 'chute in the packing shed and had charmed the SNCO in charge into letting him use it.

Having dropped my stick, the aircraft – a Hudson – climbed to the desired height as Joe checked his 'chute. As we ran into the DZ I looked out and down. I had never been up so high before. It looked a hell of a long way down. Joe took up his normal position at the door and when the green came on he made the normal static line exit – hands either side and sitting back on the haunches, the only way to get out of the Hudson door.

He made a good exit and held his position. With my experience now it amazes me to recall that he did not tumble but kept more or less upright with feet and knees together. He seemed to go a long, long way down before I saw the white puff of his parachute. Looking towards the cockpit I could see the relief on Tommy's face when he saw that everything was okay.

Joe had not obtained permission from anyone to do it. It was an off-the-cuff decision, but once it was done it was decided that all the staff should have the opportunity – but not before Gerry Turnbull. As befits the School WO, he decided that he should be next, and was in fact a little put out that Joe had beaten him to the punch. I was not present when Gerry jumped, but by all accounts, when he pulled the ripcord something went wrong. He was uncomfortably close to the ground when his 'chute developed, and it was also torn. It was decided that enough was enough, and nobody else made any free fall jumps at that time.

Alf Card

Lockheed Hudson

Haydn. *We never knew why Dad was nicknamed 'Joe'. Although Jim's later memoir supplied this clue.*

"The question may well be asked as to why one christened Kenneth should be known through the service as 'Joe'. This is particularly relevant as he always demonstrated considerable good sense and not a little business enterprise.

With the Windsor Castle taking a fortnight to sail from Gouroch to Freetown a young army entertainment officer decided that a boxing tournament would take place on the afterdeck in order to entertain the troops. This view may have been encouraged by the fact that on board was one Bruce Woodcock, contender if not the actual holder of the British Light Heavyweight title.

When Kenneth Welch casually mentioned that he had offered to go three rounds with Bruce it seemed that keeping the RAF presence had been taken much too far – Kenneth immediately became 'Joe'. We need not have been so alarmed for our colleague's safety. Despite the tropical heat this was no exhibition match and the massed army supporters rooted whole-heartedly for their man but at the end of the contest there was spontaneous and extremely generous applause for a narrow loser on points. Joe had indeed made his mark !"

Jim Averis

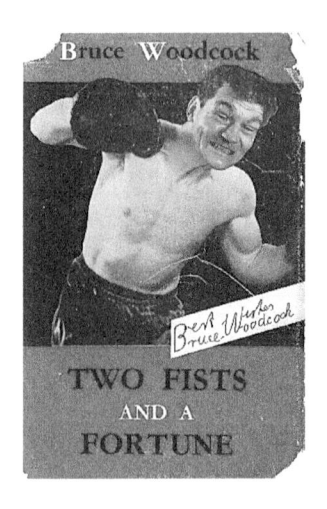

Bruce Woodcock

Haydn. When my older brother was born in 1955, Mum named him Mark but Dad always called him 'Joe'. Then in 1957, I was delivered ten weeks premature, assumed stillborn and placed in a cot whilst the doctors attended my mother for twenty minutes She needed an eight pint transfusion......On returning to the cot to deal with me and finding I was breathing, they made arrangements for an immediate christening as mother and child were not expected to last the night. Mum chose the name 'Haydn' after a childhood sweetheart who had been killed in the war after his ship was torpedoed in the Atlantic…..and whose brother, a pilot, was killed in an air crash near Kabrit. Dad had helped to recover the body.

Mum had also intended to give me 'Peter' as a middle name, after a friend of hers from Swanage who had been able to feed her information about her old flame Haydn…….and Dad. Peter worked in intelligence and had contacts. During the war Mum had attended to secretarial work for him, much of which was secret.

Sadly, in the rush and not being fully with it, Mum told the vicar it was 'Paul'. So I should have been Haydn Peter not Haydn Paul. Dad refused to call me Haydn, and he gave me the nickname of 'Jake'. I am certain if there had been other boys, Dad would have called them Jack and Jock. But why Joe, Jake, Jack and Jock in the first place? Maybe the answer is just as simple as being the names of desert companions. Whatever the reason it remains either a mystery……or a secret.

Haydn Welch

Ken wearing early PTI insignia on the left.

SAS training Bombay exits.

Joe Welch has a few stories of his own ...

Went fishing in a boat on Bitter Lake with two SAS bods (Bob Tait and Ted Badger) who acquired some very old German grenades – those on sticks with long pull-through release. Things were going fine, we had stunned and gathered in about a dozen fish when Bob stood up in the boat, pulled the string, counted the appropriate number of seconds, slipped, and dropped the grenade in about a foot of dirty water ... Approximately one in six were duds: that was one of them.

'Joner' was one of the Army instructors who had the knack of brewing up any time. He came with me when I scrounged a lift with pilot Bob Mann to fly from Kabrit to Cairo. Joner, thinking he would like a cuppa en-route turned up with Primus stove, meths, billycan etc. The aircraft was a Wellington, mostly made of wood. It didn't happen, but you should have seen Bob Mann's face. The same 'Joner' moved on to join Mihailovitch's partisans. A Yugoslav farmer had died and 'Joner' went over and assumed his identity. The farmer's wife had two kids at the time. By 1945 she had four, thanks to 'Joner.

Ken 'Joe' Welch

Bob Tait

Haydn. Bob Tait was an 'Original' member of the SAS and designed the most famous military cap badge in the world 'The Winged Dagger'. He had joined the Gordon Highlanders but then volunteered for commando training in 1940 and was sent to the Middle East in early 1941. In June 1941 at the Battle of Litani River he disobeyed an order to surrender and swam the river to reunite with Allied forces. He joined the SAS at the request of David Sterling. Bob Tait was involved in Operation Squatter being one of the twenty two who returned. He was also involved in the raid on Ajdabia aerodrome where thirty seven aircraft were destroyed.

Haydn Welch

Ted Badger at the steering wheel. Bob Tait on bonnet arm in sling.

Ken 'Joe' Welch on the sled. Kabrit.

A couple of stories from Peter Tingle ...

In Egypt we were doing a 'confidence' jump' for the troops – a stick of eight instructors from the Hudson. I was number eight. Before we jumped somebody said, "Whoever is last down gets the beers in." I fully expected that would be me, as the last man out. When I jumped, the canopy didn't open fully and was torn from apex to periphery, and several panels too, and because of this it didn't support me at all well. When I looked I immediately aged about 20 years because I knew that if I didn't do something it would be curtains. So I pulled down a yard or so of rigging line and let it go, and the 'chute opened a little more, but still didn't support me very well. Instead of being last man down, I was the first, so didn't have to get the beers in after all.

In Palestine, General Yang Chen and his Chinese Mission came to see a demonstration of parachuting, so we instructors were the dogs-bodies chosen to do this for him and his entourage. The thing to do, of course, if you didn't want to jump in a wind of 30 mph, was to get up at four o'clock in the morning and go parachuting before there was any wind. But General Yang Chen didn't know that, nor did anyone tell him, so what did we do? There we were at two o'clock in the afternoon to give him a demonstration. And was there any wind? Yes, there was a wind; it was blowing 30 mph. Not very nice at all. I personally got a bruised leg and a bruised hip, which wasn't too bad. But Tommy Taylor had a broken neck. It wasn't too painful at first, so Tommy was able to pose for the photographer with General Yang Chen and his Chinese Mission and all the other instructors, smiling merrily, before he went off to hospital to have his 'collar' put on.

Peter Tingle

Towards the end of the war, the Middle East School moved from Ramat David to Gioia Del Colle in Italy. Alf Card was amongst those who went with it ...

The staff at Gioia in January 1945 consisted of about 20 instructors, we were not overburdened with trainees. As a result, when we were not on ground training we would help with the course on their training phase. I was having a second cup of tea in the Mess and arranging with Len Berry to help him with the dispatching the next morning, when a young Sergeant came and sat at our table. He was Frankie Turner, newly arrived from Ringway. When he heard Len and I talking about dropping he complained that he had not done much flying lately so could he not fly in my place. After some good natured banter it was agreed that he should fly, and not me.

Frankie and I were great friends even though our acquaintance ship was short. Jim Seddon had dubbed him 'Tenor Turner' because of his lovely voice when he rendered popular ballads at Mess do's.

Early next morning I was roused by the sound of gravel being thrown against the window and looking out I saw him speeding away in the truck, making a victory sign as he went. At least, I think it was a victory sign.

After a leisurely breakfast I strolled up to the training area. It was deserted except for about 20 trainees. A Corporal told me that all the instructors had gone to the DZ where an aircraft had crashed. It was some time before Jack Gascoigne came back with the news that an aircraft had indeed crashed, killing all on board. Apparently it had run in and dropped a dummy, then made another run dropping an instructor, but on its next run to drop the first pair it had stalled and crashed from 800 feet. Frankie the dispatcher and all on board had stood no chance.

Alf Card

After the war, PJIs were soon active again in Palestine, in support of 6th Airborne Division's 'peace-keeping' role ...

The brief was 'Refresher courses and Exercises'. Most difficult to implement, starting from scratch. With the help of the Royal Engineers, Ringway apparatus was duplicated in a hangar. Availability of aircraft was erratic. Dakotas had to be flown up from Almaza in Egypt. Later, only the Halifax was available.

The terrorist groups – Irgun Zvai Leumi, and the Stern Gang – carried out repeated guerilla raids. The whole situation was disruptive, enough to delay my demobilization for six months.

Maurice Todhunter

Alf Card

Maurice was eventually joined by John Saxby …

My posting instructions were to report to Flight Lieutenant Todhunter in Palestine. In Cairo the RTO knew nothing about a Parachute School in the Middle East so at his suggestion I spent a few days at Shepheards while he tried to find it. He had no luck but suggested that I take a train 'about half way up' Palestine, then ask again. I chose a place called Rehoveth. Arrived there and called the nearest Army camp. They sent a jeep and we had a very good party that night. The following morning they sent me to RAF Beit Darras. I stayed the night there, had another party and then was sent on the Aqir: the headquarters of the No 2 Parachute Training School, Middle East.

Maurice Todhunter was most pleased to see me and the following night there was another party. I was much surprised to see that it was a farewell to Todhunter. Upon enquiring of him who was now in command he said "You are. I've been waiting for someone to turn up so I can go on demob."

Having thought this over for 24 hours I decided not to mention it to No 1 Parachute Training School at Upper Heyford. Thus I found myself with a jeep and driver, 2 or 3 clerks and a selection of Flight Sergeant and Sergeant PJIs and some APTC auxiliary instructors. My senior flight sergeant was Eddie Spencer, quite first rate.

We ran a series of initial courses for the 9th Battalion with much success. Our DZ was at a village called Yibna on the coast and we frequently had to clear a heard of camels off it before dropping. We jumped from Dakotas and Halifaxes including night drops and kit-bag drops and I am glad to say we had no fatalities or even much injury during my command of the School – I had first rate instructors.

Conditions could be difficult. We were always armed outside the camp and had continuous alerts in relation to the terrorist groups. In fact we usually slept with our personal weapons attached to us in bed because the Arabs were pretty good at getting in to steal them for their own use.

Shortly before my demob, Stan and I decided to find out what delayed dropping would be like, and we took a Dakota up to 10,000 feet and baled out one after the other using a P type parachute. We were told that the terminal velocity of the human body was 120 mph and I must say I spent a lot of time the night before with pencil and paper making sure to get my sums right. As I say, we jumped with P type parachutes and used our wristwatches to time the delay. Knowing nothing of stable positions we tumbled quite a lot and as far as I can remember I timed my delay for something over 30 seconds. Anyway we both arrived on the ground in good order.

John Saxby

Douglas Dakota Mark 111

4 FAR EAST PTS – INDIA

Training in India began in November 1941 at New Dehli. In October 1942, No 3 PTS moved to Chaklala …

Chaklala was 21 ½ miles from Rawalpindi, which might be called the Aldershot of India. The troops were Gurkhas, Indians, British. Great troops to train: they treated it all as a little game, and we had a lot of fun with them. Sergeant 'Chunky' Carter had this habit of getting his Gurkhas running up and down the hangar taking the shorts off other instructors and waving them in the air.

The DZ was out on the Murray Road, a large ploughed area. Dropping started very early in the morning to avoid the heat. Every Wednesday there was an instructors' stick – a full stick of twenty, very fast. We hooked straight on to the cable in the Dakota. It wasn't until 1945 when some new instructors came out from Ringway and said "You should be using strops." They nearly had kittens. So we used strops from then on. There were many incidents, on and off the DZ., some amusing, some tragic…

There was the Gurkha who landed on the roof of the Charwallah's hut during a night descent. The roof was made of mud, and he thought he had landed on the ground. So he rolled up his 'chute, walked straight off the edge of the roof, and broke his leg.

Don Campbell, jumping with an instructors' stick, landed on the back of a water buffalo, which let out a great gush of air, sank to its knees, then got up and galloped off.

Jimmy Southward decided to try a jump wearing the 'chute on his chest. He stood in the door looking inwards and got two instructors to push him out. He landed okay, but then found he couldn't reach the Quick-Release-Box. He asked a British Soldier to release him, and when asked "How the devil did you get your QRB round there?" replied, "I was trying to kick out of twists."

Impromptu concerts outside the Mess, when Jock Imerie would sing "Moonlight Shimmering In Your Hair". That's why he was always known as 'Shimmering' Imerie.

Nobby Clarke as Orderly Sergeant one Christmas day, seen wearing a pair of boots, a jock-strap and the Orderly Sergeant armband – riding a bicycle around the camp.

Chalky White was awarded the Conspicuous Gallantry Medal for a drop behind Jap lines with the Army MO to recover the crew of a crashed aircraft. *(The full story is told in a book called 'But Not In Anger' by Cole and Grant. PH.)*

Minty Eastment, a very experienced Dakota pilot, once shot up a parade of the Women's Services and left the parade ground in a dusty shambles, with females sprawled all over the place. Air experience with him was always good for a laugh. He used to dive suddenly so that the troops were all lifted up to the roof of the fuselage, then pull out and thump them all back into their seats. Burma Bill Isaacs, another of our pilots, always used to beat up Flashman's Hotel in Rawalpindi at the end of a night dropping programme to let his wife know he would be home soon.

Ron Smith

At the end of the DZ were some 'nullas', deep pits something like a miniature Grand Canyon. I never saw anyone seriously injured there but they were rather frightening. If you were at the end of a stick you pushed up and made sure there were no gaps, which could mean a late exit, heading for the 'nullas'.

Most of our pupils were Indians or Gurkhas. At the end of a course, each section of pupils invited their instructor back to their lines for a celebration. They decked us up with garlands of flowers, had a marvelous spread of food, and plied us with some unidentified spirit. As they didn't drink it themselves, they were able to watch their instructor get more and more fuddled, until he staggered back, sometimes with assistance, hoping to recover in due course and vowing to be more careful next time.

There was a campaign to shoot all wild dogs which roamed the airfield. Whilst in the training hangar one day, Trigger Bennet saw one of these pi-dogs, jumped on his bike, and whilst pedaling flat out along the perimeter track, shot the dog dead, holding the shotgun at arm's length. He wasn't called 'Trigger' for nothing!

Ron Tarry

Imagine this one told in the dry Scottish accent of Jimmy Young …

Up the road from our camp at Chaklala was a RAOC Sergeants' Mess, where we used to go quite regularly. We received an invitation to a Christmas party, so we all pitched up, and joined the fun. There was this buffet, and dancing, and as the evening progressed it was getting livelier and livelier. Taff Watkins found a suckling-pig, which we later discovered was first prize in a raffle. Taff was a rugby player, and before we knew it, there was a rugby match going on between the Army and the Air Force, using this suckling-pig as a ball. It wasn't much good as a raffle prize by the time we had finished. Taff, being tall, also pulled down all the decorations that festooned the Mess, and we wore them round our necks for the rest of the evening.

When the evening came to an end, we got hold of this Tonga to take us back to camp. For those who don't know, a Tonga is a lightweight version of an Irish jaunting-car, except that the seats are the other way round, so those in the front can see where they are going, and those in the back can see where they have been. Taff Watkins was in the front, and Chalky White and myself in the back. The Tonga wallah was on the shafts. We set off at a nice easy pace, then all of a sudden the speed became greater, and greater, and greater. I looked over and there was no Tonga wallah: no driver. Just this little white horse going at a fair old lick. I climbed over and got hold of the reins and tried to slow it down a bit. We came to the Murray crossroad. I couldn't pull the horse round so we crashed straight into the bazaar, and the whole lot went over sideways. Taff Watkins in the front thought it was great fun. We sorted ourselves and righted the Tonga, which had once had a sunshine roof. I asked Taff what happened. "Oh," he said, "I kicked the Tonga wallah off…"

We got back to camp and everyone felt sorry for the little horse, so we unharnessed it and took it into the Mess. We fed it, then went to bed. Next morning everyone was wondering how there came to be a little white horse in the Mess. "Perhaps Father Christmas brought it," I suggested.

Jimmy Young

Everyone knows the story about the Gurkhas, but it's worth repeating ...

A company of Gurkhas was paraded and the men were told that they had been specially chosen to travel in aeroplanes which would fly over the enemy so that they could jump down on them from 600 feet. The news was received in the usual stoic manner and the men were dismissed. A little later three rather nervous Gurkhas asked to see the Company Commander. The interview having been granted, the spokesman explained that they had been thinking about the jumping from aeroplanes and weren't at all sure that they could do it. They checked the height of 600 feet and it seemed too high. Would it be possible for the aeroplanes to come down to 200 feet? "But what for?" asked the surprised officer. "It's much safer from 600 feet because it gives the parachute more time to open."

"Oh, we didn't know we were to have parachutes," said the deputation in unison. "That makes it quite all right."

Maurice Newnham

In December 1946, George Podevkin, recently promoted to Squadron Leader, took command of No 3 PTS at Chaklala ...

There, among other things, we did high altitude test drops in Kashmir on to a DZ 13,000 feet above sea level.

We also carried out the one and only rescue of a trainee who had caught his foot in his predecessor's static line and was being trailed along in the slipstream. Having failed to pull him in we used, for the first time, a rather crude escape system.

The escape system consisted of: a length of rope, a length of wire with an eye-hole in each end, one shackle and bolt, a cold chisel and hammer, and two observer-type parachutes. This escape equipment was kept aboard the aircraft at all times, specifically to cater for this type of incident.

I was in the aircraft at the time, observing. I was standing just forward of the door so had a good view of the troops making their exits. No 6, who had apparently put his foot into a loop of his predecessor's static line which had been pulled out too far and was trailing on the floor, suddenly found himself suspended by this line around his ankle outside the aircraft. I immediately went forward to tell the pilot what had happened and to ascend to 2,000 feet and keep circling the DZ.

I then went back aft, and with the despatchers, tried to pull him aboard by pulling on the static line which had encircled his ankle. Despite three of us pulling, we made little headway against the strong slipstream.

It was then that I decided to use the escape equipment. I went forward again and told the pilot what I was going to do and that he was to make his run-ins over the DZ in the normal manner, putting on his red and green lights at the appropriate times. I then began to set up the equipment. The first thing was to position the two observer-type parachutes beside the door, and to thread the length of rope through their ripcord handles, through a strong point on the floor, and secure the rope in a bowline knot. I remember thinking whilst I was tying the knot that a man's life depended on it. The next thing was to thread the wire through the two 'D' rings on each of the parachutes and then, in turn, through all the strop 'D' rings on the cable. This done, one had to secure the two ends of the short wire with the shackle and bolt.

All was set. The final thing to do was cut the cable with the cold-chisel and hammer.

As the aircraft came round to make the run in over the DZ, I poised with the chisel in one hand and the hammer in the other, with my eyes glued to the lights. Red light on … Green! I struck the chisel a hefty blow which cut the wire straight away. I rushed to the door to see this unfortunate soldier hurtling towards the ground with the other two observer-parachutes entangling each other. It really was a frightful sight. Suddenly, both inflated. The shock opening on the two observer-type 'chutes had the effect of breaking the ties of the soldiers main parachute which in turn deployed and inflated, thus divorcing itself from the two life-saving 'chutes and all the other static lines and bags attached.

The soldier's ankle was sprained through being suspended by it in the slipstream. He was therefore unable to attend the final pass-out parade. He did, however, attend the badge presentation, and as he limped forward to receive his parachute wings with a broad grin on his face, I thought to myself what a lucky chap he was, and that he earned this most coveted badge the hard way.

George Podevin

The major airborne assault launched by Chaklala's pupils took place in May 1945, when the 50th Indian Parachute Brigade jumped at Elephant point as part of the assault on Rangoon. PJIs were there ...

Three of us from Chaklala were detached to the United States Air Force at Kalaikundah in the East of India - Reg McNeil, Jim Walsh, and myself. Our task was to instruct American aircrew in British Parachuting equipment and techniques. After three weeks we flew into Akyab on the Burmese coast from where on May 1st the 50th Indian Parachute Brigade took part in Operation Dracula, taking off at 0300 hours. A Path Finder Force had taken off even earlier, consisting of three aircraft in one of which Jim Walsh was acting as jump-master. In the main force which followed, Flt Lt McNeil and myself also acted as jump-masters. It was a most memorable flight for me, being in the lead aircraft, to see the whole force who had taken off with navigation lights switched on, spread out in perfect formation. It was quite a fine morning, and after flying down over the Bay of Bengal, we flew in at very low level, rising to 600 feet as we approached the DZ. The dropping went well, and we returned to Akyab without any damage or casualties

Ernie Warren

In 1946 the training of Royal Indian Air Force instructors began. In the lead up to Partition, we were employed in flying refugees into India – 60 a time in stripped down Dakotas. They were nearly all sick.

One night we were called out. Taken down to Rawalpindi railway station, and taken into a waiting room. There was a table full of whiskey, gin and beer. "Before you start what you're going to have to do, you'd better fill yourself with that. You're going to need it," said the Medical Officer. A train pulled into the station. Our job was to unload it. It was full of Hindu refugees who had been beheaded and disembowelled.

After Partition, training carried on until October 1947, when the PJIs were flown to Karachi to await transport home.

Ron Smith

The trip home in the troopship 'Dunera' took three weeks. A beautiful start across the Indian Ocean where we all acquired an authentic tan. We stopped at Aden, then Port Sudan, before heading through the Suez Canal, along the Med, past Gibraltar and up into the Bay of Biscay. We welcomed the rough weather, hoping that a number would be sea sick and leave more food for the rest of us ...

Ron Tarry

Postscript: In both Middle East and Far East theatres of war, PJIs were not only active on operational sorties: they were also involved in operational jumps.

Chaklala PJI 'Chalky' White was called at short notice to give a quick parachuting lesson to 357 Squadron's Medical Officer, Flt Lt George Graham, who had volunteered to drop into Japanese held territory in Burma to succor the survivors of a crashed Hudson. 'Chalky' not only gave the training: he volunteered to go with his pupil. On 17th March 1942 the pair parachuted into rough country close to the crash site, to which they were led by a party of Kokang guerillas. The single survivor was too badly injured to be moved immediately, and the party remained for a week in close proximity to a large party of Japanese soldiers before they were able to start the arduous journey across the mountains into China. It took eleven days of hard trekking. George Graham received the DSO, 'Chalky' White the CGM.

Being a PJI obviously wasn't exciting enough for one of the four Middle East 'Toffs' – Ian McGregor. He became an operator with SOE. During a period of nine months in 1944/1945 he made eleven operational drops into Yugoslavia to set up landing grounds. On three of those jumps he carried a dog in a harness attached to and lowered from his leg strap! He was commissioned in the field, and awarded the MC.

5 UPPER HEYFORD

Liam Forde – known as Bill in his PTS days – was one of the many who transferred from aircrew to PJI at the end of the War, and was also transferred from Ringway to Upper Heyford ...

After a long stint on Liberators (B-24s) in India, Burma and Kumming/China I repatriated to UK at cessation of hostilities in the Far East and became just another flightless bird of the day commonly known as penguins. There appeared to be millions of us, painting this, moving that.

An AMO of the day suggested that Parachute Jumping Instructors were needed and the qualification of PTI/PFO was required. With schoolboy international football and boxing credentials behind me, plus a couple of aircrew tours over enemy territory, I felt I had the stuff to become a PJI, so off I went to Cosford – then just a bunch of Nissen huts with a big gym – as a Warrant Officer aircrew, and qualified. Arrived at Ringway only to be told to take down the training equipment as PTS was moving to Upper Heyford. Took us all afternoon – spoiled the whole day.

Having commenced boxing at the age of six in Dublin, I continued boxing throughout my RAF career. I boxed several wartime and post war exhibitions with such notables as Harry Mizler (Commonwealth middle weight champ), Mark Hart (contender), Madge from the NAAFI, her twin sister Zoe, and the Tupperware lady's parachute-packer cousin ...

During my stay at Heyford (1946 through 1950), under the expert eye of the illustrious RAF Heavyweight Champion, Jack Roy, I won the 38 Gp and Transport Command Championships – many times, although I was once disqualified by JCK in one of the 38 Gp championships for persistent holding. During the bout my son Tony, then just about two years old, was heard to shout repeatedly "That's my Dad!" The innocent lad's voice got a giggle or two, but was soon joined by a chorus of PJIs and what seemed to be the whole hangar auditorium, "THAT'S YOUR DAD!" when JCK disqualified me.

I was one of 6 PJIs who went to Beaulieu, Hants, where for several weeks we test jumped the RAF's first starboard door on the

Hastings. I had a few perks when later we flew the Hastings to Hong Kong testing its capacity for litters/stretchers preparatory to the Korean fracas.

We supposedly put up a record of sorts on our last morning at Beaulieu when we all made seven descents, starboard door, between 0710 and 1100 hours. We had to get back to Heyford – it was Good Friday with a long weekend looming.

Later reduced to the substantive rank of Sergeant – aircrew ranks were by that time dismissed as a wartime anachronism – I proudly took my rightful place on the school team until my demob in 1950. We really were a great team of friends.

Liam Forde

Random recollections by 'Val' Valentine ...

Staff participation in the Station Pantomimes. Jack Roy as the 'Widow'. Jimmy Young, Fred Feast (later of TV fame), Jock Imerie, Bill Forde as either 'robbers' or 'babes'. Lofty Humphries as 'Little John'. And the not-to-be-forgotten Iris Sizeland as Alladin or Prince Charming.

When the 'poker school' was part of the training programme, with 'Dad' Stratton, 'Joe' Welch, Lofty Humphries, Jimmy Young and Bill Poyner spending many happy 'stand-by' and other hours winning or losing a few coppers – and sometimes personal effects, such as Jimmy Young's umbrella.

George (Podger) Eccles was recognized a head poacher. When resting quietly in the barrack block on a Saturday afternoon, a call came through for a trip into the woods in an attempt to retrieve a .22 rifle thrown down in the chase. To my knowledge it is still in the possession of PC Woodley, waiting to be claimed.

In July 1946 a demonstration tour with the American Fairchild Packet with sticks of sim 20s. The aircraft were based at Brize Norton and we spent the occasional happy evening in Whitney town hall where Jimmy Young would encourage the scantily dressed ladies of the 'floor show' to dance and pose before an empty camera.

A weekend trip to Butlin's Holiday Camp, Skegness in 1949 for a TA recruiting demonstration from the balloon. At midnight, after the dance, a stick of PJIs from the top board into the pool, led by Jimmy Blyth in No 1 Dress, less jacket. Next morning, Bunny Rigold having to dive in to recover stick commanders watch.

'Val' Valentine

And some from 'Olly' Owen ...

The winter of 47/48 was that bad one when we had to dig out the road from the camp towards Bicester to get the food through to us. Several feet of snow drifted around the barrack blocks. Bunny Rigold put on full flying kit – and I mean full – and jumped from a first floor window into a drift.

A man of initiative was Bunny and with courage of his convictions! Living below on the ground floor was a bunch of us slightly less exalted in seniority, and between upstairs and downstairs there was amiable rivalry. This lay dormant until suitable opportunities arose. Here seemed a suitable opportunity, maybe?

After doing a quick recce and an even quicker think, I announced brashly to my room-mates "That's nothing, you could do it bollock-naked!" Immediately several pairs of eyes swiveled on to me, with the 'Oh yes?' look in them.

When the environs were quietish, and I think it was probably dusk (it was a mixed camp then) I stripped off and nipped up the stairs with just a towel on. As I entered the room a few bods were playing cards at the table in the middle. Trying not to disturb them I went quietly behind the nearest player and said "Excuse me, do you mind if I jump out of your window?" He didn't look up from his cards, but replied absently, "Sure, carry on!"

I don't think any of them took it in. I opened the window, dropped the towel, and all they had time to see was a bum disappearing. Honour was restored to the ground floor.

I like to think of 'Dad' Stratton's voice being heard on the DZ as he gave "GO" to a stick from a Dakota. Oh yes, and there was Jack Roy holding his glass to the light and saying that there was a lot of sentiment in this beer. And at a pre-dance instructor's meeting,

Jimmy Blyth saying we had to get the number of women roughly right, to avoid too many cock-ups ...

'Olly' Owen

George Eccles used to snare rabbits. He went out one night with Bluey Lambirth to check his snares – a winter's night, snowing like hell. They wore their forage caps down under their chins the way they were supposed to be worn in winter. They were out for some time, and when they came back they were carrying – slung on a big branch, safari style – a pig. Dead. They got it into the barrack room and onto to old gas capes where they proceeded to cut it into pork joints, which everyone wrapped in newspaper and distributed to those going on leave. Everything that was left was burnt in the airmen's mess boiler room. Next morning there was a visit from a policeman, looking for a pig. A land Army girl's pet pig ...

Jimmy Young

Instructors not on courses were used on fatigue parties – carting coal about, painting around the Camp. We didn't think much of it. One morning the fatigue party was told to make up an instructor's stick. We did. We loaded ourselves with buckets, spades, brooms, and dustbins, and when we jumped we lowered them below us during the descent. Caused chaos on the DZ.

Ron Smith

After the War, the practice of attaching PJIs to Army units to give continuation training and to assist with Exercises and if necessary with

operations continued. Bill Fell was the first to command a detachment to the newly formed Territorial airborne units ...

In May 1949 JCK informed me that I was to be the first PJI attached to the newly formed 16th Airborne Division Territorial Army. The HQ of the Territorial 'paras' was in Chelsea, and was commanded by Gen Bourne (the one-armed General) and later by Gen Lathbury. Col 'Tubby' Butler, who was later to lead the Suez operation, was GI, and it was from him that I received instructions – namely to co-ordinate ground training for all the thirty-odd units, and to arrange and assist with the jumping programs. These would be mainly at weekends at Wanstead Flats and Wormwood Scrubs, although many other DZs were later added.

Aircraft jumping was restricted at first because of the Berlin airlift. From time to time the USAF laid on Fairchild Packets for us, and in return we tested the defences of their air bases. The programme meant ground training every week-day evening and parachuting virtually every weekend. Admin and travel took up the rest of my time. Life during this three-year tour was very full that I had only three actual days off – and these were to get married.

Bill Fell

USAF C-82 Fairchild Packet.

Ron Smith was also detached – with five other PJIs to Netheravon ...

Our job was to provide coverage for Airborne troops coming over from Germany for continuation training. We had no office accommodation, and our crew-room was the Orange Tree Café in Netheravon village. We had a group photo taken and hung on the wall, signed 'The Shareholders'. Some thought we really were shareholders: we spent enough there.

JCK paid us a visit and suggested we should have a Ground Training area. We tried to get the equipment from 'Stores' but were told that we were not entitled. We gave the matter some thought and one morning we took a lorry to Upper Heyford. We waited until break-time, then parked by the PTS Hangar and loaded it up with a dozen mats, a couple of ramps and several harnesses. Nobody ever seemed to miss them, and later when JCK paid another visit and saw our Ground Training area he said "A little initiative works wonders." Little did he know ...

Ron Smith

Wing Commander John Callistus Kilkenny OBE
Commanding Officer of the PTS 1947 - 1953
Known only as JCK.
Has little mention in this volume but responsible for 'Kilkenny's Circus' the procedures used in the ground training hangars and largely still in use today.

6 ABINGDON 1950 – 1965

In 1950, No 1 PTS moved to RAF Abingdon. Neither the sense of humour nor the Flight Sergeants changed ...

A certain Flight Sergeant who shall be nameless but was nicknamed 'Timber' beckons to a certain Sergeant, name of Butch Casey.
The Sergeant ignores the beckoning finger.
Annoyed Flight Sergeant says "When I go like this," demonstrating with his finger, "It means 'come here'."
"And when I go like this," replies the Sergeant, giving a Harvey Smith, "It means I'm not ******* coming."

Another occasion ... Instructors waiting in the Tower at Weston. When the message comes through that the aircraft is on its way, they all rush out, leap onto the Land Rover and jump off at intervals across the DZ, nicely dispersed, ready for the troops. The Land Rover drops Syndicate Officer and Flight Sergeant Frank Dunn at the Centre Signal. Flight Sergeant shouts for all instructors and gives the sign to double in to the centre signal. They arrive, panting. "Okay lads," says Flight Sergeant, "Spread out."

Geordie Platts

But of all those memorable Flight Sergeants of that era who put the fear of God into us young Syndicate Officers, none came bigger than 'Big Robbie'. I remember a difference of opinion he had with Bill Coad over some point of Service procedure. Both were convinced that they were right. Bill, exasperated, eventually rushed off to the Adj's office, and came back to the crew-room with a copy of Queens's Regulations. He opened it at the relevant page and banged it down in front of Robbie with a triumphant "There it is! In black and white!" Robbie studied the big book in silence for a moment, then closed it with a slam that would have taken your fingers off, and terminated the discussion by announcing firmly, "It's a misprint ..." Jimmy Young tells of a lovely tale of 'Rab' from the Ringway era ...

It was during the period when we didn't have a brevet, just that obnoxious badge of a parachute surrounded by a laurel wreath, sewn on your arm above your stripes. There used to be lots of jibes about this badge like "Are you in the RAF badminton team?"

We were in this pub and Rab was sat alongside three old ladies, and one of them said to Rab, looking at the badge, "What do you do in the Air Force?"

"I train pigeons," said Rab.

The old lady wasn't impressed, "They've been using carrier pigeons since the first world war," she said.

"Aye," said Rab, looking over both shoulders as though to make sure that nobody was listening in, "But I teach them to talk."

"Teach them to talk?"

"Aye. Just imagine a pigeon with a message on each foot, and it gets it's legs blown off. There's no message. It arrives, and there's no message."

"Ohhh ..." she said.

"Well, I teach them to talk. I teach them to listen to a message, then repeat it." Robbie kept looking over his shoulders to make sure nobody else was listening to this hush-hush piece of information.

Before you knew where you were, everyone in this pub was pointing at Rab saying, "That's the one who trains pigeons to talk."

Jimmy Young

Alf Card has other 'Big Robbie' stories ...

Andy Capp had nothing on our Rab. On one occasion he was having a snooze in front of the fire in his Quarter. His wife Rene was at work in the NAAFI shop. Suddenly Rab realized it was getting cold and that the fire needed more coal. So donning his coat and hat he made his way to the NAAFI. He saw Betty Bell, who also worked there.

"Have you seen Rene?" he asked. "She's in the store room," replied Betty. "Well away and tell her to come home. The fire needs some coal," said Rab, turning on his heels.

When the film 'The Man Who Never Was' was shown, Rab claimed to have been involved in a similar operation when he was serving in India during the War. According to him a body had to be dropped with all the evidence suggesting a parachute failure. After much searching for a suitable corpse, one was 'manufactured' using a down-and-out, and Rab had the gory task of dispatching the said 'agent'. With much embellishment he told of how he had to go over on several occasions before he was able to dispatch his, by now, rather smelly cargo.

Alf Card

Double-door jumping from the Hastings, and scrambling over the dreadful main beam in the Valetta were now standard procedures, with a little variety added by the visits of USAF C-82 Fairchild Packets ...

Dennis Leary was sent to carry out a para check on a USAF C-82 visiting Abingdon for parachute training. On his return from the dispersal he arrived in the crew-room to announce in a loud Kerry accent, "It's u/s."
 "Okay, Let's go!" said the American jump-master.
 Dennis announced again "It's u/s ..."
 The jump-master smiled. It sure is US. It's one of Uncle Sam's best. Let's go ..."
 "It's u/s! We're not going anywhere!" Dennis shouted.
This went on until someone took the trouble to explain to them the difference between u/s and US.
 I think it was on the same aircraft when we did eventually get

airborne that the USAF jump-master came round to all the seated parachutists holding out a plate full of small rubber ear-plugs. We were completely unaccustomed to such luxuries, and in fact most of the people didn't know what they were for. Doug Peacock thought he knew. You should have seen that jump-master's face when Doug put one of the plugs in his mouth and start to chew it.

Jake McLouglin

More from Jake:

Ken Kidd was acting as marshaller when Air Traffic Control phoned to say the Flight Sergeant Jack Brookes's horse had broken free and was galloping down the main runway in front of a taxiing aircraft. Ken asked if it was running well. Air Traffic Control said that it was.
"Then put two bob each way on it for me," said Ken.

Most PJIs had little time for the PT world. Nevertheless, we were still required to take the same promotion exams as 'ordinary' PTIs. Norman Hoffman came across one difficult question in the Sports and Games paper, which asked, "What is a 'fair return' in Squash?"
"Four pence per glass," wrote Norman.

Jake McLoughlin

Norman Hoffman was one of six PJIs chosen to be trained in free fall for the British Team at the 1954 World Parachute Championships. Alf Card was another ...

I remember my first 20-second delay was almost my last. We were hanging about all day as it had been foul weather and we only had a few days before we left for the competition in France. Finally the weather showed signs of improving. It was thought that the cloud base would lift to about 4,000 feet so the pundits decided that we could just manage 20 from that. Fortunately for me we managed the full 5,000 feet when we took off in the Rapide. In the stick were Norman Hoffman, Doddy Hay, Bert Shearer and one other I forget. When the time came to emplane, Doddy Hay had lost his goggles so I went in his place.
We climbed to 5,000 feet, ran in and dropped Norman, then it

was my turn. Dumbo Willans was dispatching. We clambered onto the wing facing aft, holding on to the strut with the right hand, and the door with the left hand, on which the stopwatch was strapped … At a signal from Dumbo he started my watch and I hurled myself into space. I flung my arms and legs into the required position and fell somersaulting like mad. I saw the ground, then the sky, and finally finished falling into a stable position on my back rotating slowly. I thought 'to hell with this stable position' and brought my hand in so I could see my watch. It came up to the mark that we had drawn on at 20 seconds, so I stopped it, and waited for my 'chute to open. Of course nothing happened. I realized what I had done, reached for the ripcord and yanked it fiercely. Still nothing. Into my mind came Dumbo's words about a similar situation he had experienced. I looked for my canopy and saw something white fluttering under the left side of my body, so grasping a handful I threw it away and was rewarded with an almighty jerk as my 'chute developed. Estimates vary as to my opening height. It gets lower with the telling. Suffice to say it was too close for comfort … **Alf Card**

de Havilland DH.89 Dragon Rapide

George Bruce remembers his first free fall descent ...

In 1955 I was a very young newly appointed member of the PJI staff at Abingdon. In those days there was no official free fall activity. Norman Hoffman started a free fall club using the Abingdon Flying Club Tiger Moth flown by a Master Pilot whose name I can't recall but he was Polish I think *(Jerry Schellong. PH)* The club used Weston as their DZ and for a few shillings I was a passenger in the Tiger Moth on its flight to Weston.

On arrival at Weston it transpired that there was a spare parachute as one of the intended free fallers was ill. Norman Hoffman offered me the use of the parachute and I eagerly accepted. I was given a quick two-minute course and briefing. The parachute and new-fangled reserve parachute were put on me and I found myself sitting in the front seat of the Tiger Moth.

The procedure was quite simple. I sat tight in the front seat while the aircraft climbed to 2,000 feet. On the run in the pilot tapped your head and it was time to climb out onto the starboard wing, facing the pilot. When he nodded, you let go, counted to three, and pulled the ripcord. I don't remember having been told anything about positions or what the reserve was for.

Anyway, I remember letting go, counting to three rather quickly and pulling the ripcord. There was an almighty jerk to my shoulders as the canopy deployed. There was no sleeve in those days. It was canopy first. The parachute was steerable and I had no difficulty in landing on the DZ.

George Bruce

de Havilland DH.82 Tiger Moth

'New-fangled reserve parachute'? that's right. It didn't come into regular use until 1955. Not everyone liked it. You couldn't see your feet when you were coming in for those immaculate stand-up landings.

Few, if any, can have spent more time with the 'detachments' than Stan Roe, who served with 16 Airborne Div TA, Artists Rifles (later 21 SAS), 16 Para in Egypt and Aldershot, 22 SAS in Malaya, FEAF Survival/Para, and two tours with 44 Bde (TA).

I clearly recall a certain instructors' meeting in August 1953. Instead of Landings 3 and AC Drill 2 the parachute training programme board in the corridor outside the COs office boasted a 'book' made by McCumisky on the next officer movements to 16 Para Bde. The favourite was yours truly. Why me? Could it have been that I had just bought a house in Oxford? Or had a spell as adjutant to JCK really numbered my days? My step to the meeting was neither light nor fantastic. After the usual preamble the CO said he wanted two volunteers for the 16 Para job, and in the same breath asked "who's going with Stan Roe?" Although unsolicited this move turned out to be the best in my career, leading to 24 years of continuous service in the Paras.

Stan Roe

The dramatic highlight of that career came in 1956 when Stan Roe and FS Don Birchley jumped into Suez with 3 Para ...

On 5th November 1956 Operation Musketeer was mounted from Cyprus to drop British and French paratroops and equipment at El Gamel airfield and in the vicinity of Port Said.

All paratroops of 3 Para completed an intensive synthetic ground training programme immediately before the operation, with particular emphasis on aircraft drills. Emergency procedures for crash landing, abandoning aircraft, and ditching were a feature of the training, and stick commanders were given a refresher. 720 troops were trained in 72 hours, after which PWCs were packed under PJI supervision. Because drop height was to be 600 feet there was no operational or safety purpose in wearing the reserve parachute. PJIs were allocated to aircraft with responsibility for servicing and inspecting para role equipment. They also supervised parachute fitting 12 hours before emplaning. Parachutes were then placed on aircraft seats together with PWCs. Guards were posted until take-off. It was agreed that PJIs should virtually undertake the duties of stick commanders in the aircraft to enable the SCs to give their thoughts and attention to the immediate task on landing.

At the final planning conference it was agreed sodium flares would be used to mark the re-supply DZ, particularly in the case of bad visibility. Sqn Ldr Pip Parsons, OC RAF Detachment, suggested his staff were eminently suitable for this task and Brigadier Butler fully supported him, with the main force to mark the re-supply DZ in the afternoon,

Tea was given to troops before boarding, and all emplaned on schedule. The aircraft left the marshalling area and rumbled to the runway. Line up and a brief instrument check. The ground fell below and we were on our way.

Flying conditions were smooth. Most troops settled down, some even slept, others peered through windows, but little was revealed. Two hours to go. Dispatchers gave signs as to what stage of the flight had passed. Sticks were prepared in good time and kept at readiness during the long steady approach to the DZ at El Gamel airfield. The run-in seemed to take ages but gave time to get a comfortable stance. The 'drink' was still down below when the red light changed to green. A wet reception looked on the cards!

Out – after a grimace to the dispatcher. PWC released; up with the leg strap and levers pushed outwards. The low drop height meant no messing about, and the sandy ground came up quickly. The standard of parachuting was good, especially as troops were carrying maximum loads. It reflected credit on all concerned. One paratrooper who landed on the air Traffic Control tower sustained severe bruising of his thighs, but was the only parachuting injury. This excluded those injured by enemy action during their descent, for some light ack-ack, mortar fire and machine gunning were encountered as the Hastings made their runs over the DZ.

Immediately after the main drop while 3 Para was advancing on its objectives and mopping up local resistance, I supervised the clearance of the runway, which had been obstructed with barrels, and was strewn with shell fragments. In two hours we had it ready for use. For the re-supply, we positioned the sodium flares to prevent too great a concentration of equipment in one place, and to keep the heavy stuff away from the Gamel runway. The drop was accurate and most successful. When the supplies had been collected, I was appointed by Colonel Crook, CO of 3 Para, to be responsible for all relevant liaison between the Army and RAF. We selected marshalling points and helicopter landing strips. The first aircraft to touch down were a French Dakota to pick up casualties, and a Gannet from HMS Albion with good wishes from the Navy and a most generous gift of beer and cigarettes.

We sought accommodation in the Air Traffic Control Tower. Enemy artillery had left a large gap in the ground floor wall, but the property still looked desirable, even when a fighter strafed the airfield.

Next day a Valetta, after several runs to make sure the runway was clear, landed and taxied round to B Echelon. A Wing Commander greeted the Battalion's second-in-command with a breezy "Shake hands with the first RAF Officer in Port Said". The Colonel most courteously pointed out his slight error by introducing him to me.

I continued as airfield controller, supervising the marshalling and unloading of aircraft until the RAF officially took over the airfield on 9th November. Four days had passed since that 0530 takeoff from Nicosia …

Stan Roe

The first PJI to make a trial ejection from an aircraft was Jake McLoughlin. He called the article 'Bang – You're Alive' …

It was 1958 and I was casually looking at the exhibits at the Farnborough air Show. "You seem to enjoy parachuting," said a voice at one of the stands. The voice belonged to Sir Raymond Quilter, the 'Q' of 'GQ Parachutes'.

I quickly agreed with his comment and he went on to explain that he would like the services of a parachutist to carry out ejection trials at Woomera, South Australia on a 3-month detachment. The programme was to include 5 live ejections from ground level to 40,000 feet using the 'new' Folland Gnat lightweight seat. I naturally volunteered but as I was on leave at the time I omitted to inform my service superiors and the ensuing discussions must have been hilarious particularly as Sir Raymond then contacted Marshal of the Royal Air Force Sir Dermot Boyle to make arrangements for me to be transferred on loan to the Folland Aircraft Company of which Sir Raymond was a director.

I'd already had the pleasure of leaping from many types of serviceable aircraft, through the doors, off the tail and through apertures, and the thought of going out through the roof seemed like a good idea. Martin Baker had carried out many such trials and as far as I was concerned all parachuting was extremely good fun.

Many hundreds of signals, operation orders, admin orders, and NOTAMs later found a small band of engineers, designers, a lone pilot and I installing a Folland ejection seat in a Canberra (WJ 725) at Boscombe Down. It was planned to carry out two live ejections in the UK in advance of the Woomera trial to avoid delaying the Gnat production line. The rear escape hatch was removed and the seat was duly installed in the navigator's compartment. In the preceding weeks I had made a couple of free fall jumps from a helicopter with the actual parachute to check the harness for comfort – there wasn't any!

The Canberra was soon ready for the flight, and a Javelin fitted with a cone camera was waiting to record the event. I was dressed in an assortment of gear (some for the trial, some for comfort) and a separate parachute harness was worn under the main harness with two attachments for a reserve parachute pushed through holes in the flying suit (NASA eat your heart out). I was then offered a half bottle of rum but as the oxygen mask hadn't yet got a drinking device I had to decline.

It was a relief to get moving. The taxiing out seemed like a last walk. I thought of my insurance policy which had a new clause 'ejection seat trials fully approved', and I wondered if at last I was going to make somebody rich. My only fear at this time was that when I pulled the firing handle there could be a misfire, and the thought of landing in the aircraft sitting on a 'blind' that might possibly fire on a heavy landing didn't appeal. We had therefore concocted a drill whereby if there was a misfire I would undo my many attachments and just sit in the manual opening system. Anyway, that was the plan, which fortunately we never had to use.

We were flying at 5,000 feet and 200 knots heading for Netheravon airfield. All was well and the air-conditioned open cockpit ensured that I didn't get into a sweat: I was freezing. It was a great relief to arrive at the long straight run in. I had ample time and warning to position correctly in the seat, get my head pushed firmly against the headrest and place my feet comfortably flat on the floor. The 30-second countdown seemed like a lifetime; I felt as if I were in front of a firing squad and wondered if I would hear the bang. As I sat there I wondered what I had let myself in for. I liked parachuting, but this was ridiculous. The seat felt like a dentist's chair with a live grenade rolling about underneath it. On ZERO I pulled firmly down on the blind and was aware of being compressed into the base of the seat. I took a quick look downward under the now loose blind and watched the sinister looking black Canberra fly on just a few meters under my feet. This view suddenly disappeared while I carried out 1 1/2 forward somersaults in a deafeningly silent sky over Netheravon airfield. Half way through the second somersault there was a severe deceleration while my main parachute opened. I had felt the seat separation during this time and watched it hurtle away from me with its drogue and salvage 'chute operating a thousand feet below. With the restrictions caused by two parachute harnesses there was little else to do but sit there and check the wind and drift. A stand-up landing required no effort on a stubbly corner of the airfield and my boss arrived looking more relieved than I felt. All was forgotten if not forgiven as he pushed a small bottle of Slivovitz towards me. It was the last thing I wanted but I suppose he meant well. The engineers were pleased, Sir Raymond was pleased, and I felt pretty good myself.

Jake McLoughlin

English Electric Canberra

Free Fall became official in 1959. I was one of the lucky ones sent to the French Parachute Training School to learn something about this mysterious thing called 'stability', and to begin a free fall liaison that continues to this day. The others were Johnny Thirtle, Alf Card and Tommy Maloney. I must have established some sort of record for lost ripcords, which was an expensive business, as each loss meant a round of champagne in the crew-room. The French instructors were great performers, but poor teachers. However, the mysteries were slowly unraveled, the spinning and somersaulting became less frequent. I wrote about it at the time ...

Our training was nearly over. At 15 seconds we tried turning in free fall. When stable and flat to the ground in our spreadeagle position, we were to lean to the left to start a flat turn in that direction. It worked. It worked so well that I couldn't stop it. The turn became several, and the several became a spin, and the spin a wild cartwheeling tumble through space. I yanked the ripcord early and high, and the Pyrenees revolved around me as I unwound from the twists of my rigging lines. Deniaud said that my right leg was bent; Arrasus thought it was the left; Auriole said "Arquez ... Arquez." Nicolan laughed.

On the next jump, the turns worked well, but as I was tucking the ripcord under the elastics of the reserve after the 'chute had opened, I fumbled and dropped it. In horror I watched another handle fall, dwindle and disappear. I tried to steer for the area over which I had released it, and on the ground poked with little hope amongst the long grass and heather. From afar my search was observed and correctly interpreted.

"Le lieutenant anglais a perdu son poignet!" rang out the cry over the DZ, and I was transported jubilantly to the crew-room once more.

For our last jump at Pau, Auriole took us up to 5,000 feet for a 20-second drop. We were still without stopwatch and altimeter, but counting was second nature now. It may have been rather fast counting. But it seemed a long, beautiful time, hanging in the rush of air over Pau which kept quite still for me to have a look at it in free fall. As I tucked the ripcord away – carefully, for I was broke – I grinned across at the Pyrenees, half expecting them to smile back. For a month they had watched me struggle in the sky, but then they had watched Valentin and a thousand others before me, so they probably weren't impressed.

The Commandant presented us with French airborne wings, certificates of competence, and a parting glass of wine. We shook hands with the instructors, and wished them luck. "Au revoir, mon lieutenant," grinned Nicolan, "et merci pour le champagne…"

Peter Hearn

Johnny Thirtle, Tommy Maloney, Nicolan, Alf Card, Peter Hearn

Back at Abingdon, Peter Williams was one of our early and best free fall pupils, and became deputy leader of the display team in 1962. He wrote this for me many years ago. He called it "Baby it's Cold Outside" …

The time was a cold winter afternoon in 1961. The occasion was an attempt to complete a triple baton pass with a shaving brush supplied by Norman Hoffman. Norman said he would give the shaving brush to Paul Hewitt and Paul would give it to me and a new world record would immediately be established. As this was my first sortie at the magic height of 9,000 feet, I didn't want to appear inexperienced in these sort of things and so I pushed away the visions of the world press interviewing me as the recipient of a Hoffman shaving brush in a 3-man pass and casually nodded my head as though it was something one did every day.

At flight level nine zero I still had my electric hat plugged in and was sitting on the winch when the red light came on. I had that kind of feeling of incompetence as I viewed the loose lead under my left boot and a sudden picture of everyone disappearing through the doors, including the shaving brush and my chance of world fame. To return to Abingdon would be a shame in itself and the twilight outside told me that we wouldn't go round again just for me. I tore off the soft hat and stuffed it into my overall as I ran down to join the last of the pros' and at the same time crammed my Cromwell onto my cranium, and leapt into the cold winter's evening.

Feeling like a Gerard Hoffnung character I was only too well aware that I was en-route to Weston without a helmet. It had blown straight off. The exhilaration gave way to fear. This was the day I would land on the main road and my unprotected head would become the target for some fool driver who would be looking up instead of keeping his eyes on the road. Or maybe in the wood next to Cyril Shaw's turkey farm where Bert Ancil the farmer would find me upside down banging my fragile nut against one of the trees. Perhaps a really high speed head whip from that agonizingly slow turn that only a single blank gore 'chute can inflict on the likes of me.

Instinctively I put both hands on my head, just to check. Sure enough it had gone and my head felt like an ice block. I even looked around to see if the damned hat was falling with me, like objects I'd seen in outer space films. But with eyes streaming from the cold and a deep frozen nut, I resigned myself to those fates I had foreseen moments before. At about 7,000 feet I was aware of someone close, and turned to see Paul, complete with shaving brush in one hand whilst the other was pointing to my blue head. I gathered he was trying to tell me that I had lost my helmet and I responded by holding my head. Whether or not he took this as a sign that my head was about to come off and that I no longer wanted to participate in this world-record shaving brush pass I couldn't say, because without further ado, and as though I had leprosy, he cleared off. And so did the brush and my chance of stardom.

With frozen tears and unable to see anything I settled for 3,000 feet and seemed to take ages to get into warm air to de-frost. My jaw seemed locked and down below it looked as though everyone had gone home. Fate was kind and I landed near the Wingco's car, endeavouring to hide behind the boot so that he wouldn't see my bare head. He didn't even notice, and just asked what had taken me so long.

My helmet landed near the Ben Johnson pub and a local lad brought it to the DZ. It was undamaged but for a few scratches. Hoffman said I looked strange in the air, my locks pinned flat against my head. Everyone else thought it extremely amusing. Paul Hewitt didn't say anything: perhaps he thought I was trying something new and secret. They let me carry the brush onto the coach, a sort of consolation prize I suppose. Later that evening when I told Peg that I'd lost my helmet doing a free fall she said "It's not like you to lose things, dear," and poured the tea.

Peter William

Haydn: *For some reason, in collecting these anecdotes, Peter conveniently 'forgot' to include one particularly seasonal jump as recalled by his daughter Julie:*

In December 1962, my dad and two other members of the Falcons parachute display team – Snowy Robertson and Johnny Thirtle – parachuted onto the RAF Abingdon airfield, dressed as Father Christmases. After the jump they handed out presents to children. I was four years old, at the time, and Snowy and Johnny also had children around that age. The Oxford Mail wanted a photograph of all three Father Christmases holding their happy smiling children. We haven't been able to find a copy of that photograph, but it is very clear in my mind's eye. In it, Snowy, Johnny and their children are beaming for the camera. I am glaring down my little nose at the present in my hand and Dad is looking at me as if to say what's up with you? My problem – and it seemed a very big problem at the time – was that I did not think the real

Father Christmas would be very happy about three silly men pretending to be him. It had even crossed my mind that the real Father Christmas might be so angry about this that I, myself, might not get any presents delivered to the end of my bed on Christmas morning. I got really upset about it.

Julie Hearn

Peter Hearn (centre) supported by Snowy Robertson and Johhny Thirtle. The photographer is uncredited, as he made a rubbish job for not getting the sleigh and reindeers in the image.

Julie, thankfully, also remembered this:

My father, Peter Hearn, was a founder member of the Falcons free fall parachute display team. He retired from the RAF as a Group Captain and was a much-loved storyteller in schools, and at festivals, until he started forgetting the words, and stopped.
He can still tell a good story though, about times gone by. Here's one he told at lunch today.

When Dad was in the SAS there was a house in Chelsea, close to the Ministry of Defence, where associates from America sometimes stayed and where meetings were sometimes held. Dad was there one day when somebody knocked on the door. Nobody else was expected, but the door got answered and in came a flamboyant young man. A young woman stayed, hovering on the step.

"Ah," said the person living in the house. "It's one of the neighbours. Peter – do you know Mick Jagger?"
"No." Dad said, "but I know Joe Jagger. He coached my basketball team, a few years ago, in Dover."
"Hey, Chrissie," Mick called to the girl waiting outside. "This guy knows my dad." So in went Chrissie and they all had a good old chat.

"So why had Mr Jagger knocked at the door, Dad?"
"He wanted to borrow a cup of sugar. Brown, he said, if there was any."
Really Dad? Did Mick Jagger really want a cup of brown sugar?
"That's what he said."

Julie Hearn

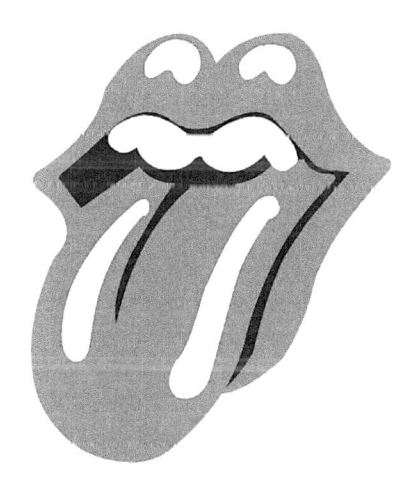

7 ABINGDON 1965 - 1975

Before he joined PTS at Abingdon in 1965, John Mace had an introduction to 'airborne initiative' from an outstanding exponent of it ...

Early in 1965, at Scampton, towards the end of my first tour as a PEdO, I met my first PJI in the shape of Flt Lt Roy 'Nobby' Clarke who had recently arrived at nearby Waddington after a very long spell on parachuting duties. I was particularly pleased to make his acquaintance because I had just learned that I was to be posted to Abingdon that autumn on the PJI course. Nobby proved to be a very amusing man with a fund of stories about PTS and its work, and a great respect and affection for PJIs, all of whom, he claimed, possessed a mysterious quality called 'airborne initiative'. Little did I know that I was to be given an early demonstration of this singular characteristic.

Both our Stations were Bomber Command and so, from time to time, we were required to attend meetings at High Wycombe: on one of the occasions I agreed to give Nobby a lift in my A35 van. However, a friend then asked if he could borrow my vehicle to move some furniture, saying that I could use his TR2 instead. The thought appealed and I duly picked Nobby up in this racy machine and we headed south. It was a very frosty day, the heater did not work properly and by the time we reached High Wycombe we were very cold indeed.

The meeting went on for longer than we had expected and as we set out on the return journey I was concerned that I would be late for a function in the Mess, since I was the Entertainments Member. Worse was to follow, because as we neared Hitchin we ran into freezing fog which caused ice to form on the windscreen and eventually rendered the wipers inoperative. As fast as I got out of the car and scraped the ice off, so it formed again, the main fault being that because the heater was faulty no warm air was reaching the glass. I remember saying to Nobby that if we couldn't get some heat on the windscreen on a regular basis then we were going to have to stop and stay the night somewhere. The latter did not appeal to Nobby any more than it did to me, but it did prompt him to come up with a blindingly obvious solution to our predicament.

"Piss on it," he said.

So I did, and sure enough it freed up the wipers and we were able to drive on for a few more miles before it froze up again. I repeated the process once more but when it became necessary a third time, I was unable to perform, and Nobby took over. He was only small and had to kneel on the bonnet in order to operate effectively.

Eventually we were both empty and it was at this juncture that I exhibited the first indication that I might have the most important quality to become a PJI. "We need a drink," I said.

So we stopped at the next pub which loomed up out of the darkness. We strolled in, demanded two pints each, sank them and marched out into the freezing night. And so we continued our increasingly unsteady progress up the A1 drinking beer we didn't want in order to generate the wherewithal to keep us mobile, until we eventually emerged from the fog somewhere near Newark. By then we were both in some disarray.

We made it back, just. I even got to the Mess, although it was the first time I had ever arrived at a function already smashed. The cold spell persisted and the next day the owner of the TR2 wanted to know why the bonnet of the car was covered in yellow ice. More airborne initiative was required to avoid telling him the truth, and so I had a head start by the time I eventually became a PJI.

But what happened to Nobby, I hear you ask. Oh, he's now a parson in Boston, Lincolnshire!

John Mace

Triumph TR2

The 'Falcons' were well established in 1968, when Geoff Greenland was leader. Early in the season, at Biggin Hill, Geoff almost ceased to be leader when he took on a Mustang with its prop turning, as he told me several years ago …

It was a misty, squally sort of day. We could only manage a hop and pop from 3,000. I was first out, out just managed to land on the edge of the DZ. It was really gusty, and before I could get the canopy down, I was off across the pans, being dragged on my backside. The next thing I knew was a sudden battering as the canopy and myself were whiplashed under the fuselage of an aircraft. When I got out, my helmet was fractured, my smokes flattened, and the canopy in shreds, wrapped round the props of a Mustang. Another couple of turns and I'd have been in there too. All I got was a busted finger, a bang on the nose, and a rollicking from Val when she read it in the papers next day.

Geoff Greenland

Ron Mitchell recalls a later free fall episode, when military techniques were better established …

Squadron Leader Merv Green, Roger Harrison, Henry MacDonald and myself, representing the Special Forces Detachment, were invited to give a display from a Wessex at Gutersloh Open day – simulating a SAS 4-man patrol using TAP Mk-4 parachutes, with oxygen and full kit. A very pretty WRAF lady requested permission to fly on the sortie and was sat forward of the door on the starboard side, out of the way. We labouriously prepared for action and Merv Green moved to the door for spotting, leaving his seat on the port side empty. The young WRAF lady decided to move for a better view and took Merv's empty seat. At P minus five seconds with red on and all stood ready for exit, three jet aircraft appeared from nowhere underneath us to beat up the DZ. Merv called 'abort', signaled to us to rest for a circuit, then sat down in his own seat – right on top of the WRAF lady. Tension was high and he shouted to her in no uncertain terms to 'Foxtrot Oscar'. Result: the young lady burst into tears and the pilot nearly jumped out because Merv had not unplugged his throat mike.

    We jumped the next time round, but the fun wasn't over. As I opened, I was appalled to see Roger Harrison going past me at a rate of knots with a perfect bundle of washing trailing behind. It looked horrible from that close! His training paid off, though. He cut away his main and pulled his reserve, and despite a heavy landing was none the worse for wear. That was one of the earliest, but by no means the last, cut-aways from the TAP Mk-4.

Ron Mitchell

The era of 'round' steerables such as the TAP series would come to an end with the introduction of 'squares'. This new generation of ram-air parachute had to go through the full Service trials procedure, of course ...

Even in the world of test jumping, things do not always go to plan and the first trial of a ram-air assembly was a monumental cock up. The age of the square dawned fitfully and it dawned in America. Throughout the '60s we learned gradually that the smart innovators on the other side of the Atlantic were playing around with gliding parachutes with some success. Here in Britain the far-sighted Walter Neumark arranged for a demonstration in the summer of 1970 of an early version of the Para Foil to MOD staffs at Netheravon. Dave Jones, then a Sergeant on the Boscombe Down Trials Team, jumped the parachute perfectly successfully but the demonstration failed to excite any military interest.

Short of a military sponsor, we persuaded the MOD Air Staff to fund a limited clearance of the squares for display uses in the hope that there would be an operational spin-off. In March 1973 I trogged off with Bob Gigg, the long-time resident brain box of Boscombe Down trials, to the Paris factory of Etudes et Fabrications Aeronautique (EFA) to buy the rigs. EFA had quickly seen the possibilities of the squares and Had negotiated the world wide exploitation rights for the 'Silver Cloud'. We completed the deal with EFA and in remarkable short time took delivery of the Silver Cloud assemblies together with their packing and servicing manuals. The manuals were, of course, in French, but in no time we had them translated into English, and the great Tom Doe, eminence grise and 'Billy Goat Gruff' of the parachute packing section at Boscombe Down had mastered the new packing intricacies.

It had taken all the team's persuasive powers to get authority for the trial at all, and even then Eric Edmunds was adamant that any live trials would be carried out using a cleared reserve parachute as a back-up. Eric resisted all my pleas to allow a 'Talisman' Reserve to be used as it had not then been given a full seal of approval: it was to be an I-24 reserve or no trial. This was to be a very significant point later.

The weather conditions on 3 July 1973 were at last ideal for the trial. The original Silver Cloud was deployed using a pilot-chute canopy control system, or 'ropes and rings' to limit the opening shock, but the system was never fully reliable in that form and the manufacturers insisted that it should only be deployed at terminal velocity. The equipment was examined minutely and I was checked thoroughly by the despatchers Flight Sergeant Peter Quinney and Sergeant Peter Keane.

The exit from the Argosy was made at 12,000 feet above Blackball Firs and the pulling height was to be at 6,000, leaving descent margin for emergencies. Our previous experience with high performance parachutes, including the interesting Irvin 'Delta' had led us to fear severe opening shocks and I therefore set myself up for the pull to give myself the best possible opening. In the event, the opening was very gentle and I found myself under a square canopy for the first time. I looked up and checked that the 7 cells were all open and that there were no difficulties with the rigging lines. It looked an impressively symmetrical sight and it took me several head-scratching seconds to puzzle out why it seemed to be going backwards. I checked again and then realized with some irritation that the whole canopy had been fitted back to front with the front of the cells pointing to the rear.

How to resolve the situation? I released the brakes and tried a few tentative turns. Sure enough, when I pulled the right toggle I turned smartly to the left and a pull on the left toggle turned me to the right. I experimented with the stall position and found that this canopy reacted much more vigorously than anything previously experienced.

There was still plenty of height for a cut-away but I was then acutely conscious that my reserve was an I-24 which was little more than an oscillating life-safer: the steerable Talisman reserve, which I had previously jumped on numerous trials, back in the packing shed. On balance, therefore, I decided that the safest option was to fly the parachute to the ground and land it backwards. I signaled to the Harvard chase-aircraft to keep me in camera and selected an inviting corn field on the northern edge of Blackball Firs in preference to the DZ which I knew was baked brick hard.

In 1973 we were sensibly cautious of stalling the canopy at critical height and I elected to maintain fairly full drive rather than risk stalling before landing. My landing was fast, vigorous and backwards, leaving a stream of dust behind me as I ploughed through the corn, presenting a dramatic sequence when the film was processed. I came to rest shaken but largely unstirred.

The DZ party were quickly on hand searching for an explanation. It was Flight Lieutenant Brian Hedley as usual who put his finger on the solution. "What's the French for left and right? Gauche and droit? It looks as if we translated the packing manuals, but not the labels on the liftwebs. They've inserted the liftweb marked gauche into the Capewell on the right shoulder and the one marked droit into the left."

It seemed that the packers didn't know their gauche from their droit. We all learned a bit about parachuting from that.

Roy McCluskcy

Armstrong Whitworth Argosy

The 'Detachments' to 16 Brigade, 44 Brigade, and Special Forces maintained a valuable link between the training element of PTS and the operational aspect of Airborne Forces throughout the period. Jock Fox, during the early 70s, was attached to 15 Battalion (TA) in Glasgow. As DZ Safety Officer, Jock rarely cancelled a drop just because there was a wee wind blowing. He would say that the aircraft could never understand him over the RT, and that he had forgotten to take any reds for the very pistols. In fact, he knew just how tough his Jocks were, and how forgiving a soft DZ can be. Jock once told me of a daylight exercise in Germany, when he was manning a DZ, armed with one of those little 'Dwyer' anemometers that gauged the wind by having it blow a little white ball up a measured scale …

The wind was pretty high. The Jocks were coming in from Scotland. The Regulars had already cancelled, and the Americans too, they had cancelled on the weather forecast and were coming in by road. Then Brigadier Pat O'Kane turns up, 20 minutes before P-Hour, and with him was this American General. They stood there watching me and Dick Watson getting everything ready, and it was blowing a bit.

Brigadier Pat shouts across to me, "What's the wind, Jock?"

So I held up my Dwyer and I said "Oh … marginal, Sir … Thirteen, fourteen knots … might just be lucky."

Well, we waited. And it was blowing a bit. Then the American General said, "Pat, I don't think you're going to get your Jock's down." So Pat O'Kane looked at me, and never said a word. Five minutes before P-Hour I told Dick Watson to light the flares, and the General and the Brigadier were holding onto their hats and looking a bit old fashioned. Then the aircraft appeared, and I gave him a green. Out the Jocks came, and they piddled across the sky … Anyway, they landed, then UP, and away! Marvelous. It was soft, you see.

Pat O'Kane called me across and still holding his hat said, "Not bad, Jock. By the way, what IS the wind?"

So I took out my Dwyer again and said. "Oh, thirteen knots, Sir, just on the borderline," and the American general says "Let me look at that instrument. How does the goddamn thing work?" So I says, "Well, you just hold it up to the wind and the wind blows through this little hole and pushes a little white ball up and down this tube so that you can read off the wind strength."

"Does it?" he says. "Oh yes," I says. "Let's have a look," he says, and he and Pat O'Kane stood there holding this thing up and staring at it for about a minute. Then Pat O'Kane says to me, "Where's the little white ball?"

"Oh, I forgot to tell you," I says. "I lost the little white ball out of it three months ago."

Jock Fox

Ron Mitchell recalls another DZ incident ...

Exercise 'Hellenic Express' in the mid-70s. Three DZs to be covered in a 'milk run' drop from C130s. The work up to P-Hour had been thirsty work, with all DZ parties consuming their fair share of 'Retsina' in local Greek villages. John Parry, one of the three DZSOs, was fast asleep in his tent when he was woken in the early hours of the morning to be informed that it was 5 minutes to P-Hour. JP grabbed trousers, boots and radio, leaped aboard Land Rover, and headed frantically for DZ. He got the signals down just as the aircraft crossed the DZ threshold. The aircraft Captain broke radio silence to inform DZSO that the signals were the wrong way round: JP had laid them on the reciprocal bearing. The drop was successful, and from that day JP was known as 'Wrong-Way Parry'.

Ron Mitchell

I know of only one officer who was accused of being drunk in charge of a DZ, but funny things can happen on a DZ at night, even when you've only been drinking Coca Cola ...

The Tuesday 'milk-run' to Everleigh DZ started as it usually did, with a 08.00 hours departure from Pitts Road. The essence of this story is as clear in my mind as if it happened yesterday, yet it occurred almost a pension time ago ...

Tedium, excitement, peaks and troughs are what PJIs learn to expect early on in their jumping careers. This day was no exception. The long hours between the 10.00 hours drop and the 23.00 night descent were only highlighted by the usual excellent lunch in the Sergeants Mess at Lyneham, and by meeting there a few ex-PJIs who eschewed poverty of rank to seek higher echelons in the world of the 'Air Loadies' – a traumatic decision for many PJIs in the era of transition. I am going off-track from the main point in my story, but 'off-track' is the keyword.

To kill time and thirst we called in at the Everleigh local. It was warmth and convivial company for the cost of a pint, though as driver, I was restricted to 'coke'. 22.00 hours saw us on the DZ with an easy hour to prepare for P-hour. Then the routine of laying out the goose-neck flares for the Approach, Centre Signal, and Stop Drop bar; checking out the radio and the pistol-signal-2" with cartridges red, yellow and green. All ready!

Now the last minutes to wait before the drop. I checked my watch in the light of the Centre flares – one minute to go, eyes back to the sky and the line of the run–in track. Yes – there she was! 1 x Hercules with sixty troops on board – but off course to starboard by at least 100 yards.

I thought of the troops who had been standing, Prepared for Action, for at least twenty minutes weighted down with equipment, pressed, hard to move ... What effect would the course correction have on them? Close to cursing and chaos, without a doubt.

With this thought came the visual shock of seeing not one, but two sets of lights, on a parallel course. The horror of the situation – the probability of an air collision churned my stomach. I shouted a warning to the DZ Safety Officer. I could now see the bulky outline of the Hercules, but of the other craft alongside it there were only the lights, no shape, no indication whatsoever of the type of aircraft now taking such a risk in flying in Restricted air space. Now, and directly overhead, the troops started to spill out of both doors of the Herc. Still fearful of collision, I kept sight of the other lights. On reaching the centre Signal, they suddenly changed to vertical flight, at a speed I have never seen equaled by a helicopter, or for that matter any fixed-wing fighter. In seconds the lights receded to pin-points and then nothing. The Hercules was still disgorging troops.

With troops to check, equipment to retrieve and stow aboard the Land Rover, there was no time for comment on the incident. Later, at the wash-up, everyone in the ground party agreed that they had seen what I had witnessed.

The possibilities of lightning or aircraft intrusion were later discounted. A flying saucer? Don't ask me. All I know is that PJIs are pragmatic in most aspects, and do not readily suffer from hallucinations. Particularly when they've only been drinking 'coke'.

Harry Appleby

Our 'resident' officer at Weston On The Green during the latter years at Abingdon was Peter Burgess ...

As a thank-you for allowing him to use the peri-track for access to some of his land, a local farmer gave me some day-old chicks, which got me started in the poultry trade at Weston. The next step came when, as a joke, I accused villagers of being rustlers. They didn't have quite the same sense of humour as us. They called an extraordinary meeting of the Parish Council, and agreed to present me with a pair of geese, which were duly and ceremoniously handed over by residents of the village. Bleep and Bloop the geese were called. Their moment of fame came during a CO's inspection, carried out by Group Captain Bill Green, Station Commander at Abingdon at the time. He had the usual entourage of administrators and DOE brass. Bleep and Bloop didn't mind parachutists, but they took an instant dislike to DOE, whose reps were to be seen, halfway through the inspection, in full flight across the airfield being pursued by two irate geese. When Bill Green stopped laughing, he called off the inspection and we went to the crew-room for a pint of his favourite Worthington 'E'

Peter Burgess

Most of the Medical Officers appointed to look after the physical welfare of the PJI have taken great and lively interest in us — such as 'Doc' Winfield of Ringway days, and 'Doc' Johnson at Abingdon in the early 60s. But not all the Doc's appear to have been on our side ...

During the early '70s at Abingdon the SMO was a fat Wing Commander who seemed to have a distinct dislike of PJIs. At the end of his annual medical, Flight Lieutenant Les Evans was being debriefed by this gentleman. Now Les was, and still is, a very heavily built man, but in those days most of his bulk was made up of solid muscle resulting from regular weight training, Les having been a Welsh international weight-lifter.

"Of course, you are overweight," said the good doctor who was most certainly so himself.
"Oh dear," said Les, in his lilting valleys accent.
"Yes. What's the lightest you've been?"
"Seven pounds, three ounces," replied Les.
"Get out!" screamed the physician.   **John Mace**

An unusual airborne operation in 1972 involved a bomb-disposal expert, two Royal Marines, a member of 22 SAS, the liner QE2, and Flight Sergeant Terry Allen. Nobody else at PTS or RAF Det Special Forces knew what was happening. Neither did Terry Allen until he was on board the aircraft. What followed was a fine example of PJI initiative – recorded in his official report.

At 1340 (on 18 Mar 72) the two Royal Marines and myself took off from ATURM in a WASP Helicopter and flew to RAF Lyneham, where I met the S/Sgt from 22 SAS. At 1500 we boarded the C130 which I immediately checked for parachuting role. The aircraft started up whilst I was carrying out the checks and we moved off – stopping somewhere on the pans to pick up Captain Williams, who had apparently just arrived by C130 from Abingdon. Also brought aboard were various items of bomb-disposal equipment. This was lashed down and we took off at 1535 hours.

When we were airborne I spoke with Captain Williams who I knew from a past meeting, to be informed that somewhere at sea was a large ship with a bomb on board and that he and his equipment were to be transferred to it. I discovered that his parachuting experience consisted of 3 static line descents as part of a free fall course, and half an hour's ground training for a water descent at Abingdon with Sgt Ball, who had travelled with him and was also on board.

On sorting out the equipment that had to be dropped I estimated that the total weight was over 200 lbs and included detonators and explosives was extremely bulky. In addition to this there was the personal clothing of the four parachutists. We set out to make up two loads, the plan being that two men would parachute on the first run with the equipment and on the second run Captain Williams would be No 1 with Lt Clifford as No 2 in clean fatigue so as to be able to stay near him to give assistance in the sea in case of difficulties.

The loads turned out to be extremely bulky and heavy – far beyond the limits laid down in SOPs. There was also the question of buoyancy. To be on the safe side I attached a passenger life-jacket to each load with the red operating handle uppermost, and instructed the two parachutists to operate this prior to releasing the load after development of the parachute.

During the flight I gave Captain Williams further instructions on water descent procedures and he seemed to grasp exactly what was required of him. In addition I discovered that a shotgun had been put on board and that this also had to travel with them. I decided it would not be too inconvenient for Lt Clifford to carry this and still be able to offer assistance to Captain Williams in the water. The gun was stripped and parceled up in plastic bags and using lashing tape was attached to Lt Clifford by a body line.

At one stage while preparing the equipment I went to the flight deck to attempt to have a briefing with the pilot, but I could not get near him. The flight deck was crowded and I was informed that he was too busy accepting and passing messages, but I spoke with OC Ops RAF Lyneham and he put me in the picture what was going on.

At 1800 hours we prepared for action and were at Action Stations at 1900. As we flew in it was discovered that the cloud base was down to 500 feet. After orbiting the QE2 several times I was asked if the parachutists were willing to jump from 800 feet instead of 1000 feet. I agreed to this on their behalf and we then proceeded to do several dummy runs – coming in at 500 feet, climbing to 800 feet in a short steep climb and leveling out. Nobody told me they were dummy runs, and we were at Action station waiting for the lights throughout. Each time the manoeuvre was tried we suffered negative G and became airborne at the open door.

Due to the size and weight of the equipment, I had Sgt Bell on the forward side of the door supporting the parachutist. On the green we were to concentrate on assisting the equipment out of the door, the parachutist to make an exit as best he could. During this time I noticed that Captain Williams was starting to look ill.

At 1930 the green light came on after completing another fast climb manoeuvre and we managed to get the first two parachutists out. I saw their parachutes deploy then they were swallowed by the cloud. I signaled Captain Williams and Lt Clifford forward and hooked them up. Immediately Captain Williams was sick; all over me. I arranged for a cup of cold water to be brought aft and this he drank.

We then started for the run in and I found myself supporting a very sick and nervous man. Just as the QE2 came into view the ALM shouted that it was to be a dummy run. I shouted back that we would never get Captain Williams out if there were to be any more dummies. This must have been understood for the reply was

115

that it was to be live.

The green light came on. I forcibly ejected Captain Williams through the door. Lt Clifford followed him out fast. I saw both their parachutes deploy and also the shotgun disappearing through the cloud, having become separated from Lt Clifford ...

We later had confirmation from the QE2 that all the parachutists were safe.

Terry Allen

Peter Hearn and Doug Peacock. Abingdon March 1973

8 BRIZE NORTON

A great feather in the cap of PTS was the training to 'wings' standard in 1978 of two VVIPs. Eddie Cartner, as OC Basic Training Squadron at the time, was responsible for the training – anxiously watched, as you can imagine, by every level of command above him …

By a happy accident of posting date I was serving at PTS when a senior and exceptionally public figure was to pass through our training system as a student. Not too far removed from the Throne of England, and better known than most to Her Majesty, he was bringing his younger brother along too. Unable, in the timescale of decent posting interval, to dislodge me, my masters were obliged to accept that perhaps under close supervision I might just carry off the task without affecting the dynasty. With some alarm, but enormous pride I prepared my training squadron for a once-in-a-lifetime opportunity.

During the period leading up to the 'Royal Training' it had been decided that the OC Basic Training Squadron and each of the selected personal instructors to Prince Charles and Prince Andrew would go to meet them to establish a rapport, do some ground training, and even try some kit.

On 1st March 1978 Sergeant Steve France and I were required to report to Queen's Flight at Benson from where we would be taken to Gordonstoun School where Prince Andrew was in his final year. Steve and I were a little taken aback to find that the flight would be in one of the highly polished Andovers, but in true PJI style, managed to give the impression that it was a fairly routine event.

We climbed on board the gleaming machine, barely recognizable as a working aircraft, and took our seats in what seemed to be a drawing room. A Warrant Officer steward in starched white monkey jacket arrived to see to our seat belts. Group Captain Miller, Deputy Captain of the Queen's Flight boarded, the engines started at once and we were airborne – it all seemed a bit rapid compared with our usual experience in the back of a 'Herc'.

Alone in our drawing room, Steve and I considered our lot. Coffee in bone china was served and biscuits on fragile plates appeared; it was a 'best blue' trip, so perhaps we were only being given attention to match our turn-out. Over Durham the urbane Warrant approached again. "Would you care for a newspaper, Sir?"

Steve, immaculate in 'No. 1s', highly bulled boots, and just getting his first 'roll up' going, took it like a real professional. Leaning back into the deep upholstery with a satisfied nod he said, "Yer. Have you got The Sun?"

Having convinced my RAF masters that our most important student of the year at PTS would be attending the course as a Colonel of the Parachute Regiment, all that remained for me to do was sit back and wait for the 'normal' course of events to unfold. Surely PCAU would see to the pre-course admin. I'd forgotten about our earlier hints that some preliminary ground training would be to everybody's advantage.

So it was that on the eve of annual Air Officer Commanding's Inspection I was telephoned by somebody sounding suspiciously like a page from Debrett's who said, "The Colonel would like to have some of your pre-course training after all. Can you manage that tomorrow, at ten?"

"Er …. Yessss … Er, er …."

"Jolly good. Tomorrow at ten, then. At the Castle, of course. Good bye."

It was just as well that my caller had rung off as I would doubtless have demonstrated my complete grasp of events by asking something essential like 'Er, which castle is that, then?'

As my Sergeant and I headed East in the morning we soon saw the Heathrow departures passing over the Colonel's place and so steered directly for it. Met with courtesy and efficiency we were ushered through into the inner courtyard; the police clearly recognizing some secret signal invisible to us. Smartly saluting an elegant civilian gentleman, just in case, we were finally shown into an ancient lift built of polished mahogany and beveled glass. This decanted us alone in the upper reaches of the place where we were met by the Colonel and his brother. Resisting the ridiculous urge to say 'The face is familiar, haven't we seen you on the Telly?' I burst into my pre-training litany which ended lamely with "We'll need somewhere to practice some parachute rolls."

It seemed such a daft request considering the size of the place. Nothing daunted, the Colonel led us off at a fast pace along bewildering corridors and stairways until we entered a vast hall of perspective-stretching dimensions lined with frames of stained glass and mahogany. Incongruously there was a ladder behind the door, which sight restored my failing grip on reality.

"Will this do?" asked the Colonel.

"Yes, I suppose so," said Sergeant Glan, an imperturbable Welshman showing no signs that I could detect of any nerves at all. Dashing off to our Service Chevette standing in splendid isolation in the courtyard, we began to tug rubber mats up to the hall. We were helped by a man in a kilt who appeared as if by magic; hadn't one of the Colonel's forbears ordered kilt-wearing at some stage? Very soon, encouraged by Sergeant Glan's example and only slightly modified PJI language, the Colonel and his brother were happily rolling about the floor in an approved manner. Occasional members of staff, attracted by the din, beat hasty retreats when they realized that their master was not actually under threat.

After the mat-beating, my contribution did not quite match Glan's when I discovered the 3-pin-square-semi-detached plugs did not quite match 2-pin-round-centuries-old castle sockets, and the Colonel was obliged to squint at the slide presentation by holding each one up to the light.

Sweating with our combined anxiety and physical efforts we were delighted to see that the Colonel was puffing a bit too, but was delighted with his hours work-out. We lugged all our mats back to the car and departed. Something, however, was different. Crowds had filled the courtyards and now lined our poorly remembered escape route. Not to cheer us, surely? Had the fame of PTS spread so far, so quickly? Flustered by the peering faces we made a left turn only to arrive in a quiet avenue barred by an iron gate. Beyond this one of the Colonel's soldiers stood post. He was facing away from us, but we were trapped! Beyond his immaculate and immobile red shoulders we could see ordinary life proceeding without us. Facing the crowds again, staring rigidly ahead and above all not waving, we retraced our route, and suddenly saw the front of the soldier – we were out!

Sergeant Glan produced a huge cigar – a real baby-celebration monster – and, giving vent to his true feelings at last, he gasped,
"Permission to smoke, Sir?"

Eddie Cartner

Throughout its history, PTS has continued to export its training skills. One of the most recent Schools established and manned by current and former PJIs is that of the Sultan of Oman's Parachute Regiment, where Jake McLoughlin served for a while as CO …

A new 'Fan' trainer had been installed. The Arab PJIs seemed to have great difficulty in co-ordinating the release of the cable drum with the exit of the pupil, so that on some occasions the drum was unwinding while the jumper was still in the door before he got to the end of the loose cable. There was a hell of a whiplash sound and a serious kink appeared in the cable.

I stopped the programme, got everyone around me, and through an interpreter gave a lecture on the procedure and the serious effect such a malpractice could have if the cable snapped. I showed my displeasure, and heads nodded in agreement. Those concerned were Omani PJIs of varying experience. I asked for comments and questions. One older NCO asked if the cable could be used again. I pointed out the frayed and sharp ends on the kinked cable and told him it could not be used again for such training.

"In that case," he said, "Can I have it to tether my goat?"

Jake McLoughlin

In 1982, our Airborne Forces went to war, in the Falklands. And our PJIs went with them.

It was 1550 hours on 13 June 1982. We were 51 degrees South, the Hercules on Airdrop ELAINE had been flying for eleven hours and the call came "Prepare For Action". The troops of B Squadron 22 SAS shrugged out of their sleeping bags, put away the books on advanced astro-physics, marked the page of the Sunday Express Puzzler, and started to concentrate on the matter in hand.

The whole operation still had an unreal quality about it. Only weeks previously I had been sitting in the office in high good humour reflecting that for the first time that I could remember during my tour, all of the training officers Brian Hedley, Brian Morris & Geoff Diggle were in London at the same time, and even John Read had managed to stop off for an hour or two between tasks chasing 22 SAS around the world. Spirits were high and the level of noise was in direct contradiction to the lofty level of policy matters under discussion, when the banter was interrupted by Warrant Officer Keith Teasdale announcing that he had a No Duff call for me from a Captain Curruthers RN at the MOD Ops Cell.

"Hello. I'm the duty Operations Controller at the Ministry of Defence and I have been given your desk as the officer who can advise me on mounting a parachute assault. We can authenticate later, but for the time being am I in the right court?"

"Probably, Sir, but can you give me some idea of the parameters of the task? Is it operation or exercise? Military free fall or static line? Is the delivery platform rotary or fixed wing?"

"Well, first things, first, this is for real, it's no exercise. Beyond that, I'm a submariner, old boy, and I haven't a clue about any of the other points. If you assume we want to put in almost one hundred troops, how long would it take you to get the resources together?"

"Okay, Sir, I'll assume that they are all trained troops wearing either sand or green berets and I will have the resources and PJIs available to you at any port or airhead you nominate within 24 hours."

"Grand. You plan on that basis and you'd better make sure your men are ready for cold weather."

We had been hearing vague rumours in the media about odd scrap-iron deals in South Georgia, and heightened tension in the Falkland Islands, but a hundred paratroops to be ready in 24 hours seemed a bit precipitate. However, in the absence of any clearly defined MOD staff imperatives, we decided just to get the job done. Within minutes Keith Teasdale was able to tell me that warrant Officer Hitchcock at Parachute Support Unit Hullavington had reacted with his customary phlegm and gave assurance that the war reserve store was open, kit was available, and he would deliver where ordered within 24 hours. After that things flew. The camp beds were laid out in HQ (Chelsea), and planning went on round the clock. No practical contingency plans had ever been worked out and the ramifications of operating against Argentina on an offshore island some 8,000 miles away were only beginning to be appreciated. Serving both Commandant Ground Royal Marines and Director SAS, we at RAF Detachment Special Forces were right in the thick of things from the start, but there were no convenient plans that could just be drawn from the files and dusted off: we were starting from scratch.

Deep into the nights of Easter weekend we drew up plans for airborne assaults against the enemy, realizing that the difficulties of location, weather and distance from the UK would provide formidable problems. Meanwhile, Flight Sergeants Doug Fletcher and Bob Roberts embarked with the Task Force in HMS Fearless to look after possible helicopter operations and many weeks later performed heroics in flying helicopter missions in advance of the landings to survey possible assault beaches by thermal intensifiers – airborne initiative to the fore as usual.

As the Task Force steamed south the RAF Det SF staff devised, practiced and refined a quiver of parachuting options using static line, water drop and military free fall techniques. The training was intensive and John Read's team at 22 SAS – Flight Sergeants Bill Cooke and Chris Buchan and Sergeant Des Desbois – were re-writing the SOPs as they went along. They plotted low level, high level, mid-level, and remote-control stand-off parachuting and several variations in between. Sadly, in the middle of the training, John Read picked up a problem on his 'square' and crashed to the ground, smashing his pelvis. The imperturbable Geoff Diggle was, therefore, drafted in as we moved south to Ascension Island to start the final flush.

Ascension in Spring 1982 was of course little more than a permanently manned aircraft carrier. When we arrived, Flight Sergeant Norman Austen was already holding the fort with the advanced party. It was readily apparent that any paratroop operations to be mounted from Ascension would be SF tasks, and Norman returned to the UK leaving the RAF Det SF team to work with B and G Sqn SAS and 47 Sqn SF Flight.

The days on Ascension soon settled into dull routine, punctuated by daily heavy-drop and paratroop sorties to the battle front on the Falkland Islands. Both SAS troops and RAF PJIs were striving to fight off boredom on our desert island, yet we were only too well aware that within hours we could all be winging south on 24 hour long sorties to the battle zone. It was a soul-wrenching sight to see poor Des Desbois choking back the tears as he drafted his will for the tenth time. "It's not the dying that bothers me," he moaned. "It's just the thought of being parted from all my hard-earned money."

It became pretty much a ritual that each night before a sortie the troops going south would be entertained to a pre-battle party with one of the several Fijian warlords of 22 SAS as master of ceremonies. The flights south were expensive and complex, involving air to air refueling of the Hercules by Victor tanker aircraft, so those who were airlifted were by definition troops who were very special to the order of battle. There was a steady stream of SAS troops, Signals Specialists, and - memorably – Lieutenant Colonel David Chaundler, plucked from the security of a Ministry desk to take over command of 2nd Battalion Para Regt after Lieutenant Colonel H Jones was tragically killed leading his men into Action at Goose Green.

Through it all, B Sqn became increasingly anxious to get a share of the honours and it was with a sense of profound relief that the Squadron emplaned for takeoff just after midnight on 12 June in two Hercules for airdrop ELAINE. The monotony of the 11-hour flight in fearfully cramped conditions had been broken only by the drama of the mid flight refuel. As the host Victor Tanker positioned in front, our captain Flight Lieutenant Iain Molyneu linked the probe unerringly but, despite two greens, the Victor failed to supply the fuel. On five separate occasions we chased the Victor down the sleigh ride with equal accuracy but with equally fruitless results. In the end the aircraft parted and we called up a reserve Victor to give supply.

But now we were within an hour of our drop to HMS Glamorgan, and the troops were preparing for action … The Drop was to be into the Antarctic Ocean, and for many it was to be their first water descent ever. There was an air of contained excitement, even exhilaration, as the troops struggled into the unfamiliar rubber 'dry' suits as protection against the numbing Antarctic waters. Des Desbois worked methodically through his troops reminding them in his mock-morose fashion that the birds were all coming home to roost now, and that they would be wishing they had spent more time in continuation training jumps and absorbing his pearls of wisdom on parachuting that they had sneered at over the years.

"You'll soon learn if you haven't got it right," he muttered to each jumper as he meticulously checked assemblies. At the same time an enormous Fijian warrior solemnly presented each soldier with a Fijian war slogan to wear as a headband, which he had painstakingly painted on lengths of lashing tape. He seemed to be in ecstasy of anticipation.

The navigator gave us the ten-minute warning and the tailgate swung open to reveal flurries of snow over the forbidding inhospitable ocean. If anything, the sense of exhilaration increased as the troops realized the jump was on. The battle equipment was dispatched over the edge in advance to the lonely Glamorgan, illuminated by welding flashes as the ship was repaired after action with the enemy.

The aircraft started its final run in for its live drop. The troops tensed as they were given "Red On". I felt my left elbow being grasped, and a very large, beaming Fijian face was pushed close to mine. "Boss, this is the greatest joy of my life. I am parachuting into battle with the greatest regiment in the world – AND DES DESBOIS HASN'T CAUGHT ME FOR SYNTHETIC TRAINING FOR THREE YEARS."

At "Green On" he fairly leapt over the edge, and into war.

Roy McCluskey

Handley Page Victor refueling Hercules C130 South Atlantic

In 1983, to create a permanent record of crew-room comments and quips, the 'PTS Line Book' was introduced. Following are some of the printable entries

During the 1984 PTS Cocktail Party the Chief instructor was talking to GP Capt Jimmy Blyth.
"Do you remember meeting my mother, Sir? You went to the same school."
"Christ!" says Jimmy. "I'm not your father, am I?"

Overheard in the hangar: "When you have fitted your jettison device, ensure that you put your tongue through the elastic band."

Overheard on command PA at Weston during an inky black night descent: "Watch the ground and assess your drift …"

Overheard from a non-para PEdO: "He may be okay as a PJI, but could he cope with a responsible job in a gymnasium?"

Flight Lieutenants Bown and Allison were questioned by a member of Free Fall Training Flight, "If your altimeters are set at 200 feet left, what does that indicate?"
Flt Lt Bown: "The DZ is 200 feet below sea level."
Flt Lt Allison: "There's a 200 foot slope on the DZ."
Nevertheless, they both became successful 'Falcon' leaders!

Mick Threlfall to Barry Henderson on arrival at Weston for regular course night descent: "Barry, have we got a moon tonight?"
"No – but I can arrange one if you like …"

Flight Sergeant May at Brize Norton, talking to WO Thomas, visiting from Aldershot: FS: "What are you doing here then?" WO: "I've come to have my teeth seen to." FS: "Couldn't you have sent them?"

Flight Commander to Syndicate Officer: "You ought to cut down on the swearing. It's not becoming of the officer on a course. Leave it to the NCOs – we can't compete with them anyway. I've got an excuse 'cos I used to be on the other side of the fence, but you don't need to do it." Syndicate Officer: "Yeah, okay Ginge. Now F*** Off – I'm busy on the Fan next …

9 1990 AND BEYOND

And the last word from Brize Norton and from the Parachute Training School in its 50th year quite properly comes from the School's present Commanding Officer, Wing Commander Peter Watson ...

As we enter the 1990s, PTS continues to flourish. It does so largely because we retain an important training and support role, remain very busy, and still manage to go away to faraway places and return with smiles on our faces! On re-reading Peter Hearn's Preface, I am reminded that this 'anecdotal history' is, rightly, a mixture of humour and memories. Necessarily, though, the last words should perhaps include a quick look into the future.

In this context, we see an increasing number of training courses and tasks, multi-skilled PJIs who are (even now) subject to categorization checks, and rationalization of the PTS detachments so that we can serve the many arms of Airborne Forces to even better effect. In addition to the strong links that we retain with Commonwealth countries, we also enjoy an increasing involvement with our NATO colleagues on both sides of the Atlantic. But overall, we are part of what is happening in the RAF as a whole. In particular, 'Estates Rationalisation' is with us, and that means movement of units so that some of the older inactive stations can be closed and sold rather than refurbished at enormous expense. I hasten to add that PTS will certainly continue to function, but we may move from our present home at Brize Norton and we may have to use an alternative site for all that currently goes on at Weston-on-the-Green. But, enough of the future; let's return to the present, in more light-hearted vein, and to the subject of PJI humour in the School's 50th Anniversary year.

Peter Hearn reproduced some of the printable entries from the OTS 'Line Book', but here are a few gems from the 'Sales and Wants Book'!

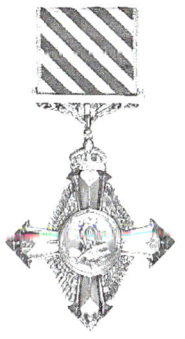

Peter Hearn upon the presentation of the Air Force Cross

Power of School WO:	*For Sale:*	Electric 'Qualcast' SE 30X Rotary Lawnmower. One yr old, good condition. £40 (no nearest offers) *Contact:* Sgt Greg McKenzie SNCO IC Exercises. Working weekends and Guard Cdr duties.
Post Script:		"And now Orderly Sgt duties! Signed N E P AUSTEN WO School WO"
Marriage:	*For Sale:*	Good for the wife. Six months membership to 'In Shape Health Club in Oxford' - £65 Signed Sgt Simon Jay Training and Standards Flt.
Post Script:		"What about yourself?"
Support Staff:	*For Sale:*	Present OC Training Co-ordination and Resources Flt. Going cheap due to years of wear and tear. Several parts worn out and needs good servicing. Open to offers! Signed: Helen and Pam (and probably Sandra, too!)
Post Script:		George Sizeland's response is predictable!
Revenge (again Support Staff):		Wanted: Plates for use in crew-room to replace those taken during the last Station Exercise. Signed: Marion

It's a great privilege and honour to be OC PTS in its Golden Jubilee Years. I'm particularly grateful to have been given the chance to round off Peter Hearn's magnificent overall effort to put events and memories of the last 50 years down in highly readable format. Here's to the next 50 years!

Peter Watson

Peter Hearn BA, AFC, RAF (R'td)
31 August 1932 – 14 December 2021

PART TWO

10 HAYDN

Haydn. *In adding to Peter's work (reproduced in the first nine chapters and now concluded), the rest of this volume is written on behalf of all those PJIs whose stories remain to be told. Peter Hearn got the start right through his collection of anecdotes forming this work, "There I was at 500 Feet". How to end the tale is a different matter entirely. How do we tell the story of the men who taught the men to jump, since they no longer teach and no longer jump?*

I have chosen my dad, Ken 'Joe' Welch as the last of "The Four Toffs", to represent the men who should all be remembered. For many, the years spent jumping are long gone, but these pioneers, servicemen and heroes lived on. Most of whom had families and loved ones. These tales are their tales and stand to represent all who jumped. All had a story to tell. What became of them? History has failed to say. But maybe, one by one, their stories can be told.

Firstly, let me introduce myself and a little later to my younger sister Lorna. We were Ken's youngest children. Let's see how Dad wove his life with ours after he dispatched his final stick and in keeping with the anecdotal experiences collected by Peter Hearn, I have a couple of my own to tell.

It was inevitable that one day, I too would jump. It was always something I wanted to do and the chance came whilst at college. It was 1975 where I saw an advertising poster stuck on a notice board for Dunkeswell International Skydiving Centre and a phone number to call. It was that simple. Since that day, I have realized that many journeys and adventures, whether short and simple or long and complex, can begin with that one phone call. I made the call and within a couple weeks Dad dropped me off at Ian Loutitt's School where I had booked a two day course. The first day ground training and the second day a short refresher and two static line jumps.

It was such a thrill, aged 18, climbing aboard a Cessna 172 with a parachute strapped to my back. During the twenty minutes it took to get to height, 2,500 feet, I knew without any shadow of doubt, that if the parachute did not open, I would forget the emergency drills, and simply die.

It was slightly disappointing to realize that the order to jump, was no longer, "Prepare for Action ….….. Action Stations …. …..GO"

"PREPARE FOR ACTION"

"ACTION STATIONS"

"GO"

but the rather bland "CUT" (telling the pilot to cut the engine), "BRAKES" (telling the pilot to apply the undercarriage brakes), followed by a heavy tap on my shoulder. Then finding myself looking out of a gaping hole in the fuselage (where a door had once been), at the undercarriage wheel, onto which I was required to place my left foot………..... I remember it very odd to focus so much attention on the wheel, whilst the beautiful Devon countryside was out of focus 2,500 feet below. Then with my left foot now resting on the wheel, my left hand reaching out of the door and grabbing the wing strut, I pulled my body out of the door and in one very swift movement reached out with my right hand to also grab the wing strut, and trailed my right leg into the void.

There I was at 2500 feet, outside of an aeroplane, underneath the wing and holding onto a wing strut. Thinking of it now, it still seems ridiculously adventurous compared to just jumping out. Then came the one word "GO". I jumped. Yelling so loudly I am sure they would have heard me from the ground, "One thousand, two thousand, three thousand, Check Canopy".

Never had I experienced so much joy when looking up and seeing a perfectly formed round parachute above my head. Oh, and the serenity starkly contrasting with the sheer panic of moments before. It was stunningly beautiful. Pulling gently on one toggle and the parachute rotated, then the other toggle and it turned back. Pulling harder, it did the same but faster. After a few short minutes flying the parachute, whilst embracing relief, peace and joy, came a new and urgent realisation, the ground is approaching rather more rapidly than expected. Another short period of terror ensued thinking I might land on a fence. The landing hurt more than the practice landing falls, but the smile was bigger.

The second jump an hour or so later was no less exciting with the added touch of having repacked the parachute myself, before the jump.

I made eight static line jumps at Dunkeswell and then moved to Cambridge. I had in fact handed in my notice where I worked in an Exeter jewellers (more of that later), to move across the road to a competitor for an extra £15 a week. I had earmarked this money to fund flying lessons. As it happened, when I explained to my area manager the only reason I was leaving was because I wanted to fly, he suggested whether doubling my salary would persuade me to stay, but the job was in Cambridge. It would be a temporary assignment whilst I received more experience prior to managing their Kings Lynn branch.

    Explaining to Nicola that I was moving 200 miles away was pretty horrid, but it worked out perfectly in the end. She moved too and got a job in a different jewellers two doors away.

 I called in at Waterbeach Parachute Club, eager to make my first free fall jump before switching to flying lessons. After four more static line jumps, performing dummy ripcord pulls to simulate pulling for real, my new instructor cleared me for my first free fall. It would be jump number thirteen.

    Waterbeach operated a Cessna 206 so the exit was not made by climbing out, but simply sitting on the floor of the aeroplane with legs swung out into the slipstream, and the jump was pushing myself from a sitting position straight into the slipstream. The first free fall was as incredible as the first static line jump, but with a greater awareness of events. My whole being no longer suffering from sensory overload, I was able to comprehend what I was doing. On the word "GO" I jumped. At the count of three thousand I reached for my ripcord, and pulled it on the count of four. It took much more effort to pull than expected and the extra couple of seconds taken for the canopy to inflate was quite noticeable. It certainly felt like I was falling. A real thrill and I wanted more.

    One of my Waterbeach jumps didn't quite go to plan. Maybe it was my fault or maybe the instructor's for not checking. Everything went well, until the landing. I felt I was getting good at them. The ground rush, the timing and the roll. But this time it hurt… real bad… It seems I had not tightened my leg straps, and when my weight under the parachute transferred to the ground, the webbing between my legs went slack, and as I rolled I experienced a sharp squeeze. It made me wince. On the way home I made an unannounced visit to A&E. The doc asked me to drop my trousers so he could take a look. One testicle had swollen to double its size. He said, "Go home and rest them on a velvet cushion for a couple of days, but not to worry because you have two. It would be a different matter had you only one".

Then one day, Nicola asked me to marry her.

Haydn & Nicola 1979

It wasn't the first time a loose strap caused some bother. I was jumping with my longtime friend 'Big' John Mellor. The day before my wedding in 1979. John had made a number of jumps whilst in the police and came to stay for a few days. We popped up to Dunkeswell. He was No 1. I was No 2. John was a big lad. Probably too big. Having climbed out of the aeroplane he could not make the correct position in the fairly cramped space between the wheel, strut and overhead wing. But there he was, in the slipstream under the wing, poised to jump, more or less in a crouching position rather than a standing star. On the command, he jumped, threw his head back and formed the classic stable arch with arms and legs in a star shape. I didn't hear the thud as his head hit the underside of the starboard wing, but the impact knocked his helmet clean off. It didn't really matter much, until he came to land, and as fate would have it, 'Big' John landed on a section of concrete. None the worse for it. The next day, the morning of my wedding, we returned for one last jump before the service,..........it was too windy.

Another day at Dunkeswell. I was No 2 and due to exit the moment another policeman had jumped. The policeman messed up his exit by stepping onto the wheel with his right foot, which meant he could not properly swing out and hold onto the wing strut. For a moment he hesitated whilst I could only watch him try to resolve the matter by grabbing the wing strut with both hands and then trying to hop his right foot along the wheel to make space for his left foot. Sadly he mis-judged it and hopped off the wheel completely. There he was at 2,500 feet dangling from the wing strut with both arms at full stretch and looking back into the doorway with the look of 'what do I do now?' Clearly, all he could do was let go, but he still waited for the command "GO".

There are some things you do when at the time you are doing them, you don't realise that it will be the last time you will ever do that thing. Like when after being walked to school, you kiss your mum goodbye at the school gates….did she ever realise then, that that kiss would be the last time she would be kissed at the school gates? I guess the time would come one day for my last jump and this day was that day.

Moments before boarding the aeroplane back at Dunkeswell, Ian Loutitt did the obligatory equipment checks. On checking my 'chute, he did not like it, the pack appeared rather lumpy. He had me remove the pack, and he passed me another. He explained the ripcord was in a different position and was smaller. Rather than being a large D shaped handle (big enough you could grab it with your whole gloved fist) on my right side above my waist….. This handle was a small round thing in front of my right breast under my shoulder.

Whilst the Cessna engine was running, I rehearsed two or three jump backs, star spread position, look at my shoulder (not my right side), reach for the handle and recover. We climbed aboard.

In all my jumps, I never really enjoyed jumping from low heights. Everything always seemed too urgent, too rushed. I much preferred jumping higher, even for short delays. But today cloud base was low and we barely managed to find 2,700 feet as we flew through the base of wispy clouds during the run in. The usual instructions, "CUT, BRAKES", the tap on my shoulder and out I climbed. This would be a 'hop and pop'. No long delay just jump and pull the ripcord. "GO", I jumped. "One thousand (form stable spread position), two thousand (hold position), three thousand (look for and grasp ripcord), four thousand (pull ripcord and reform the stable spread position), five thousand, (wait for the jerk of the canopy as it opens and check canopy). Except this time nothing happened.

I didn't bother to look around wondering why I couldn't see a perfectly formed Double L parachute above my head. In that split second, I knew I had not actually pulled anything. Muscle memory caused me to look at my right side, reach and grab an imaginary non-existent ripcord, pull and recover. This time, my hand was empty. The ripcord still snugly sat in its un-seen position in front of my right breast.

It only takes 23 seconds to fall 2,700 feet before you hit the deck and I had already spent about 6 or 7 of them. I looked again for the ripcord, still forgetting it was in a different place. But there, on my belly, right in front of my gaze, I saw a lovely large handle. I grabbed it, gave it a sharp pull. Billows of beautiful white nylon spilled from the reserve pack and disappearing in an instant, between my legs. A loud crack and the 'chute opened. What a glorious sight, smaller than expected and non-steerable. I floated down for a minute or two, whilst drifting backwards in the wind.

Many student parachutists complained in those days, believing the jump was what it was all about and the bit under the canopy was boring in comparison. I always disagreed. Flying a parachute was always a lovely contrast to the few moments before, and this jump proved it. Those that thought the bit that made the landing safe, was dull, only had to buy one of the new 'square' parachutes. Then they could throw themselves about the sky to their hearts content............if they wanted more thrills.

The ground was getting close and I had that foreboding feeling that things were not quite over. This became more obvious as the peaceful tranquility was destroyed by the loud throttle-up of an approaching light aeroplane. I was drifting straight down the centre line of the live runway and the aeroplane, well into its final approach, had to take avoiding action. Goodness knows how the pilot must have felt suddenly becoming aware of a parachutist opening too close for comfort and wondering whether there was room to continue his landing or to go round again. Thankfully he aborted and I prepared to land, which was rather awkward as looking over my shoulder hoping to drift across the runway and land in the grass, it was clear I would not get across. The landing was further complicated by the oscillating of the canopy. I didn't quite get the timing right and hit the runway with a thump, partially still swinging backwards. I crumpled into a heap.

My instructor was pretty cross. Not so much for the jump, but he was the only person qualified to pack emergency 'chutes.

Driving home, I knew then, I had just made my last jump. It was 1980 and my wife Nicola was expecting our first child. It was another decade before I started flying lessons.

Ken 'Pegasus'

Big John and I shared many adventures without relying on parachutes to save our lives. We sometimes relied on each other. Variously taking long kayaking journeys down the River Wye, hiking the South West Coastal Path in winter and hitch hiking to the Isle of Skye to rough camp for a week.

Our last adventure being in 1992. I was swimming the frigid waters of Loch Lomond as a competitor in the longest distance swimming race in British swimming. Big John, Mark Pardoe (my wife's brother) and Tony Henley, were my escort crew, taking turns rowing a boat alongside me as I swam the 21 miles. Fifteen hours into the swim, John encouraged me to give one last effort to finish the last mile and it looked like I might win the race as only one other swimmer was still in, the others all having retired. I apparently said, "I don't think I can swim that far". John ordered me to take his hand and as I raised my arm to grab his, I sank.

I don't remember John pulling me into the rowing boat, setting off the emergency flare, transferring me to the rescue boat, reaching the shore or the ambulance ride. Thankfully, neither do I remember the young nurse who was asked to remove my grease covered Speedos. I do remember waking up all warm and cosy in Alexandria Hospital, in Glasgow a few hours later. A doctor came to see me, saying, "I have sent people home in a box who were far warmer than you." He was surprised I had made it. Big John saved my life that day and looking at the video, I certainly did not have another mile of swimming in me, possibly just a few more minutes.

Two weeks later Big John and his wife Karen were on a plane emigrating to Canada whilst I was swimming the English Channel. Over the next 25 years, I met up with John just twice more during his visits back to England. Then in 2019 we heard John had cut his big toe whilst kayaking. The cut had not healed and he was in hospital having his toe amputated. The operation appeared to have gone well, but John died the following morning.

Big John

11 KEN

So, what of my dad? Dad, the man of whom it was said (by him) that Hitler trembled when he heard the name of the 'Great Ken Welch' 'Joe', the last of "The Four Toffs".

Kenneth Francis George Welch was born in March 1918. His birth mother Jeannie Johnstone, gave Ken up for private adoption, straight from birth, to my Granny Welch who was a nurse and a friend of Jeannie. Jeanie was one day short of her 30th birthday. The adoption was forced upon Jeannie by her disapproving parents. Whilst Dad's birth certificate and adoption papers stated his mother's name, the father was not mentioned. He remained a complete mystery, a secret.

Along with the adoption papers, a secrecy bond agreeing no contact would be made between the families, was signed. A substantial £500 penalty was agreed should the families break the terms of the agreement. (As children, we understood Dad's father was a wealthy army officer of some repute, but we were forbidden to discuss it). When Dad found out he was adopted, aged fifteen, he ran away from home for a week, until his money ran out.

Dad had two dreams. To fly and to box in the Olympics. Joining the RAF, he thought, would put him on the path to fulfil both dreams. In 1938 and surprisingly for a man with an ordinary working class upbringing, no university education, no military heritage, no wealth and certainly lacking the posh accent, his application was approved and he commenced the selection process. Sadly for him, during the various selection processes prior to flight training, his application failed. Dad was colour blind (it seems the other Toffs also failed to fly for similar reasons).

How Dad even got as far as applying to be a pilot begs questions, unless maybe his application was somehow 'favoured', directed from afar or otherwise watched over. With his dreams of becoming a pilot dashed, he turned to his other dream, to become an Olympic boxer. He took the position as an Aircraft Hand and immediately he passed basic training he transferred to be a Physical Training Instructor and won the Inter Services boxing championship that year.

Then the war came and spoilt everything, until Churchill made a life changing announcement. In 1940 Winston Churchill requested a corps of 5000 paratroops. Louis Strange, former WW1 pilot became the first Commanding Officer charged with forming No 1 Parachute Training School. He chose Jack Benham as his second in command and Chief Training Officer. Benham was responsible for writing the training manual to help them figure out the best way to teach the troops to jump. Designing modifications to aircraft and equipment and devise systems and schedules that could manage the training of hundreds of troops. The decision was made that RAF Parachute Jump Instructors (PJIs) would be selected from the existing teams of Physical Training Instructors (PTIs). In June 1940, Dad volunteered for an assignment of a 'hazardous nature' and was one of the first RAF PTIs to be selected. He had no idea he was volunteering for parachuting. Those chosen were told to keep the posting a secret.

Having alluded to the idea that maybe Dad had a person of military influence watching him as he grew up and who may have watched over (maybe even facilitated) his application for pilot training. I wondered whether Dad's dad was closer than we might ever have thought.

Having recently had a DNA test, I was surprised to learn of a substantial percentage of Jewish DNA which could only have come from the unknown side of Dad's ancestry. The test result indicated a family match to a German Jewish family with the surname of Elkan. At the time of these results, this was just a surname. Until, quite out of the blue a long while later, I realised that Dad's superior Training Officer and ultimately Commanding Officer at Ringway was Jack Elkan David Benham. I was immediately drawn to him, as coincidence is often not far from the truth. Could Jack have been Dad's father? Might Jack have been keeping an eye on Dad's childhood from afar and monitoring (even mentoring) his progression in the RAF? I needed to find out how close Jack's connection was to my dad, if indeed there was one.

The journey revealed an unbelievable story of chance, red herrings, dead ends, intrigue and coincidence as my wife Nicola took it upon herself to spend the covid lockdown in research to find out, "Who's the Daddy?"

12 WHO'S THE DADDY ?

Ken 'Joe' Welch

Jack Elkan David Benham

Ferdie Elkan

Harry Elkan

Jack Benham was born in 1900 to Lionel Benjamin and Mabel Elkan. After Lionel died, Mabel and Jack changed their surname from Benjamin to Benham presumably to distance themselves from their German Jewish ancestry. Between the wars, Jack had joined the family cigar business owned by his Grandfather Alexander Elkan. It was Jack that designed the livery and logo of the Montecristo brand of Havanna cigars which they had sole rights of import.

Jack's mother, Mabel Elkan had a sister, Daisy, who was the managing director of court milliner Ann Talbot Ltd. Ann Talbot Ltd made dresses and costumes for Queen Victoria's court and latterly King Edward V11. Her businesses partner Elsie Petre was also a regular at court and became a member of the Prince of Wales's 'set'. Elsie was rumoured to have been one of Edward V11's many mistresses. She used her connections in the theatrical world as well as her connections in court which enabled Ann Talbot Ltd to make costumes for ceremonial occasions for the Royal Courts where women and Debutantes were presented to the Queen. *(This is where the coincidences start to make your spine tingle)*, Elsie Petre's father was William Clark, the rector of St Mary Magdelene Church in Hammet Street Taunton. (Hammet Street, Taunton was where Granny Welch who adopted Dad used to live). Somehow a link to Benham was becoming very real.

It didn't seem much of a stretch to wonder whether a seventeen year old Jack might have got into a little trouble with Jeannie, an older women, resulting in the adoption. Might Jack then have kept a watchful eye on Ken?

Looking further and from a different angle, Nicola found this: Shriener Wolf was born in 1799 in Germany and emigrated to England. He married Matilda and they had twelve children. Three of their daughters married clockmakers (all bothers). Harriet Wolf married Walter Samuel, Emma Wolf married Alfred Samuel and Rachel Wolf married Henry Samuel. Harriet Samuel became the H of H Samuel the well-known British High Street jewellery retailer.

Being a retail jeweller myself, this too caught my eye wondering if or how Jack was related to the families of H. Samuel. I imagined a scenario of my applying to manage an H. Samuel shop. The area manager might ask, "Why would you like to work for H. Samuel?" I would reply, "Because I am family."

However, it is Rachel and her husband Henry that caught my eye more. They had a daughter, they also called Harriet. *(Here comes the next coincidence that makes you shout "No Way").* Harriet married John Elkan who was the brother of Alexander Elkan (remember him?) He owned the Elkan cigar company that Benham became a director of between the wars. Alexander was Jack Benham's grandfather and the father of Daisy Elkan who made dresses for Queen Victoria's court and whose business partner Elsie (who may have slept with King Edward V11) and who as a child lived in the vicarage in the same street where Granny Welch lived, who adopted Dad. That Daisy Elkan's sister was Mabel, who was Jack Benham's mother. (Family history research makes you repeat things from different directions, it helps you get your head around it.). Certainly the plot thickens full of intrigue and mystery.

Then there was this newspaper report of 1917, the year of Dad's conception, *(my comments in italics).*

"Captain Clarence Elkan D.S.O a member of Field-Marshal Sir Douglas Haig's staff *(Douglas Haig was the Commander in Chief of the British Army)* at general headquarters, has been promoted to the rank of Lieutenant Colonel. With the office of Assistant Quartermaster General *(which is one of the more senior positions in the British Army).* Colonel Elkan is a son of Mr John Elkan *(the jeweller and brother of Alexander Elkan, Jack Benham's grandfather),* and nephew of Mr Edmund Itzig Julius Elkan. Mr Elkan's second son Herman *(Harry)* has been gazetted to Captaincy in the Dublin Fusiliers."

We always knew from the beginning that Dad's father was a wealthy army officer, whose name was to be kept secret. Might Clarence be the daddy? Was Dad the skeleton in his closet? Was he the reason why the father's name was to be kept secret? Or, as often happens during family research, do we find ourselves running down rabbit holes, finding red herrings, dead ends and more questions. Were Jack and Clarence just another rabbit hole despite the coincidences.

All this conjecture and wanting it to be true does not help. Family history research is not just about proving things, as much effort should go into research that might disprove things. But for modern DNA testing this might have been the closest we could get.

It was this Edmund Itzig Julius Elkan, claiming (in the newspaper article) to be the uncle of Clarence, and Edmund's father Sir Julius Elkan who was my DNA match.

Sir Julius Elkan, Privy Counsellor, Knight Commander of the Order of the Bear and his son Edmund (a cigar importer) and who (if Clarence Elkan was indeed Edmund's nephew), proves Jack Elkan David Benham was related to Dad, but was not his daddy. If we could have told Dad that Jack Elkan was his second cousin, he would have been thrilled at the revelation and said, "Get on ! "

We have not yet been able to prove whether Clarence was indeed Edmund's nephew as suggested in the newspaper cutting. Although it seems highly probable that Clarence and Jack would have known each other as they were cousins, what we needed was to find evidence that places either of them in a romance or otherwise, with Jeannie, Dad's birth mother.

However, in continuing to answer the question, "Who's the Daddy?" My wife Nicola looked further at Edmund. Edmund was a German Jew who emigrated to Australia in 1875. He married and had four sons, two of whom (Harry and Ferdie) were in England in 1917. It has to be said, that Ferdie has a remarkable family likeness to Dad. Sufficient for us all to declare he must be the daddy. This likeness continued through mid and old age, in all stages of their lives they look a perfect match. Ferdie's Australian war record suggests he was a 'ladies' man'. Indeed, letters possibly from jilted lovers were written seeking his whereabouts. Although Ferdie married, he had no known children, maybe he was the daddy or maybe by 1917 was unable to have children.

Harry on the other hand already had one child out of wedlock before the war whilst still in Australia. (Perhaps he too was a 'ladies' man, especially if he also fathered Dad during a war time romance in England). Harry had joined the Dublin Fusiliers and was badly wounded at Gallipoli. He spent six months in hospital at Alexandria before being sent to England to recuperate. In England he was placed on a Special List and transferred to the RAMC (Royal Army Medical Corps) as a surgeon dentist (before the war he was a qualified dentist). In the RAMC he specialised in anaesthetics for those with facial injuries and reconstruction requiring dental work. Sadly the records for his service in England were largely destroyed in bombing raids and so it is hard to place him in Plymouth, which is where Jeannie lived and worked during WW1. After the war Harry took up dental practice in Egypt and attended to King Farouk. He married his childhood sweetheart and eventually returned to Australia.

In Australia Harry's dad Edmund wanted to adopt Harry's illegitimate daughter but would only do so if there was evidence she was really Harry's daughter. It was her dental records that gave this proof, she had the same genetic tooth anomaly that Harry had. Coincidentally (or evidentially), Dad and all of us children also have this same tooth anomaly, where one or more adult teeth fail to grow. It seems that Harry may be the daddy after all.

We needed to find a way to connect Harry or Ferdie with Jeannie. We know that Jeannie worked in two hotels and could easily have met a number of soldiers staying there. She also performed on stage and had a 'sweet contralto voice' and that Harry also loved the stage. Might they have met in that way? Of course, we may never know the truth of it. But the coincidences don't stop. What of Jeannie, Dad's birth mother? What happened to her? After the war, she married………..her husband was a surgeon dentist in the RAMC.

So returning to the original questions, how on earth did Dad have his application for flight training approved (despite it ultimately failing due to being colour blind)? Was he being watched over? Were Jack or Clarence Elkan aware of him? Did they also know of Ferdie and Harry their cousins? What was the extent of the family scandal requiring an adoption straight from birth and bonds of secrecy drawn up?

One thing is certain, if there were other unknown children out there and any living family members submit a DNA test to find more of their ancestry and heritage, we will get more tantalising clues in our search to find out, 'Who's the Daddy'?

Sadly, some months after taking command of the Parachute Training School at Ringway, Benham was dispatching some SOE over Belgium. On the return trip, engine failure twenty miles off the coast, caused the Whitley to ditch in the English Channel. Benham was killed, aged 42. There were no survivors.

13 BACK TO KEN

Having been training the troops at Ringway for a year or so, Dad once again volunteered to go on another hazardous assignment. Prior to leaving, he went home to tell Mum. She was not at all happy.

Dad and Mum

They had only been married for two months before he went to Ringway (and during that time she had no idea what he had been doing or where) and now around one year later, he was telling her he was off again. He was supposed to be home for two weeks, but due to bad feelings and arguments he stayed for two days, before storming out. She did not see him again until March 1945. He did however leave her pregnant with my eldest sister Juliet.

Dad, (so the official story tells) along with three PJI mates Mac, Jim, and Natch, embarked on the troop ship the Windsor Castle, not knowing their destination but assuming their mission was something to do with setting up a training program somewhere, as they had sufficient kit to train an army. There is some confusion whether the original destination for the new school was supposed to have been India and Benham was to be posted there as Wing Commander. However he failed the medical as unfit for a tropical posting and stayed in England to specialize in dropping SOE. Whether destined for India, the Middle East or somewhere else, the four RAF PJIs found themselves without a Commanding Officer and sharing the troop ship with mostly Army personnel.

Windsor Castle circa 1941

Jim Averis takes up the story.

"It was the persuasive manner of an old time Company Sergeant Major, whose wizened features portrayed long service overseas and who confessed to having operated illegally behind the grandstand at Kempton Park who began it all. The Sergeant's mess quarters on the troop ship Windsor Castle were a series of closely packed three tier bunks somewhere below decks. After the official "lights out" this CSM would appear with his Crown and Anchor Board (a three dice gambling game), install himself in the middle of the largest available space and generously invite one and all to join him and be a Toff. Not merely a Toff but a lucky Toff.

Whether it was felt by the four RAF instructors en-route to the Middle East that it was incumbent upon them, in an almost exclusively army mess to uphold the "we'll have a go" spirit of the RAF, or merely misguided thoughts of easy money, at least three of the four would fall each evening to the blandishment to be a Toff. The call persisted amongst the four long after they left the Windsor Castle at Freetown. The now familiar phrase "The Middle East Toffs", owes everything to that delightful character on the troopship and his persuasive patter. Many may feel that as "The Four" are now preparing for the 50th Anniversary in January 1992 of their first course at Ringway, they are indeed "Lucky Toffs".

Jim Averis

Ian 'Mac' McGregor, Jim 'Ginger' Averis, 'Natch' Markwell, Ken 'Joe' Welch
"The Four Totts" Kabrit 1942

"The Four Toffs" RAF Brize Norton 1992

Haydn: At Freetown "The Four Toffs" disembarked, taking a small boat and slipped unescorted along the West African coast. Travelling to Lagos and staying two weeks at the Carter Hotel. A canoe ferry to Apapa and eventually taking a three day flight in a Dakota (landing before nightfall for two stops) to Cairo. Cairo to Kasfareet by train where more non fare paying passengers were clinging to the outside, than fare paying passengers were inside. Then by small truck to the SAS camp near Bitter Lake at Kabrit. Dad always said he was not sent to Kabrit, but that was just where they ended up.

At Kabrit, the "Four Toffs" found the troops had all been posted. There was nobody to teach except a few disparate bands of men and partisans. ....and Col David Stirling on the prowl.

The story goes that Dad first met Paddy Maine in jail in Kabrit. Both were in separately for fighting. With Dad taking bets on him boxing all comers in the ring. Both being international standard boxers, they got on famously.

The fact that Dad and the "The Four Toffs" were not just RAF Parachute Jump Instructors but actually knew of the whereabouts of enough parachuting equipment to train a small army, did not go unnoticed. Paddy Maine had exactly that, a small army. Whether the school was destined for India or the Middle East, nobody cared. Stirling had been asking Ringway to send instructors for ages, having previously tried and failed to teach themselves to jump. Stirling could now try again, properly. Shortly after "The Toffs" arrived in Kabrit, the Windsor Castle had to make an unscheduled stop at Suez for repairs. The parachuting equipment might well have been liberated and in any case, never made it to India. 'The Toffs' were shortly joined by six Army Parachuting Instructors under Sergeant Major Johnny Dawes. India would have to wait and No 4 Middle East Training School would (around twelve months later) be regularised and the official records appropriately played with.

Jim Averis recorded:

"It happened about a month after our arrival. The four were sharing a comfortable ridge tent with wooden framed beds. Relationships with the SAS were such that practical joking was always a possibility. Joe's skills as a boxer has already been mentioned, that he was tough may be guessed from his schoolboy nickname of "Cast", abbreviated from cast iron !

Joe found bed bugs quite impossible to cope with. He solved the problem by 'winning' a sheet of corrugated iron which he bent to form an open-ended trough, placed it on bricks and slept soundly for two nights.

Such bizarre behaviour could not possibly go unnoticed or unrewarded. On the fourth night as Joe in all his nakedness but carefully clutching his pest-free sheet, stepped onto his bed. There was a report that reverberated around the corrugated iron like a ship's mini broadside, whilst Joe beat the standing high jump record. Foolishly thinking the boys had done their worst, Joe, determined no doubt to show that such frivolity could not delay his slumbers, once again stepped boldly onto his bed. The result was again devastating, and for at least twenty minutes the pantomime act continued; it seemed no matter where Joe tried to get into his bed at least one detonator would go off.

It was a long time before Joe felt that he could actually lie down without causing an explosion. Many were the guffaws that came from the neighbouring SAS tent but Joe, always generously big-hearted, was by the morning well able to enjoy the joke. Indeed within days he went of his own free will on one of the SAS pre-selection hikes designed to sort out the weaker brethren. Needless to say Joe acquitted himself very well indeed." **Jim Averis**

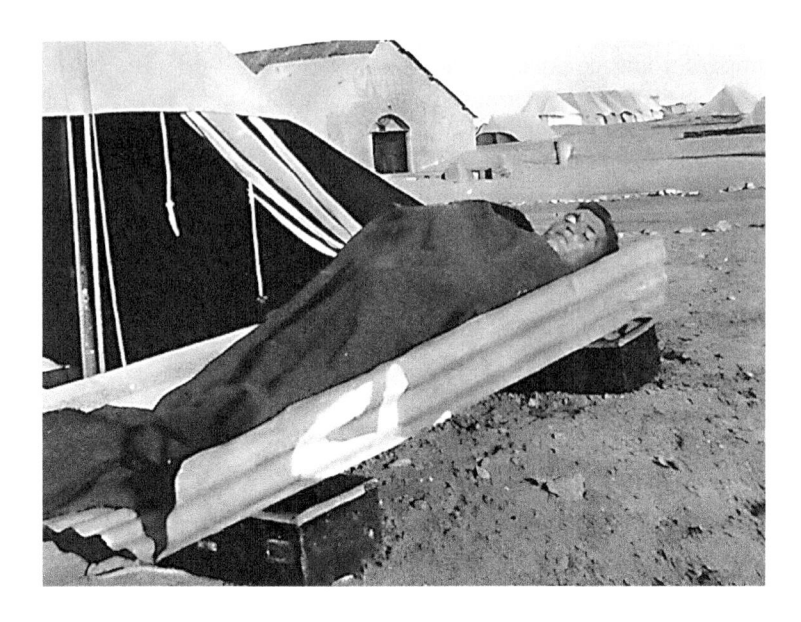

Ken 'Joe' Welch

Haydn: There are many official reports of the things the SAS and LRDG got up to in the desert. Although sadly, the role the parachute instructors played seems to have been ignored, particularly by the SAS. Only in recent works do we find details which (as family members we have known since childhood) have been researched and the stories are only now beginning to be told.

"The Four Toffs" commenced a training program to teach the SAS to jump. British Pathe News shows Dad astride rigs being towed across the desert whilst troops are jumping off the back at high speed. Prior to this they were trying to teach themselves by jumping off the back of speeding Land Rovers, making some quite dubious landings.

Then the day approached for Operation Squatter. Stirling's bold plan to drop fifty five SAS troops behind enemy lines, which on the day had increased unofficially to sixty five.

Quoting from the excellent Damien Lewis book "SAS Brothers in Arms"..............
"Accounts differ as to what exactly was said at this juncture. There were dissenting voices. Sergeant Kenneth 'Joe' Welch was a

parachute jump instructor (PJI) who'd been sent out from England to assist with airborne training at Kabrit, and to help get everything ship-shape for Squatter. As he pointed out, if the wind speeds were anything like those forecast, the Bombays shouldn't even fly, let alone anyone attempt to jump. In such conditions, 'chutes were likely to collapse and men would die. As Welch made his arguments, some seemed to be swayed, agreeing that maybe it was too risky. The debate became extremely heated, and Welch was forced to declare that they may as well jump without parachutes, for at least that way they would die clean and quick".

As fate would have it, when Squatter commenced on 16 November 1941, five antiquated Bombay aircraft each carrying 15 crew and paratroops took off. Dad was the dispatcher on David Stirling's aeroplane, three of the other four Bombays carried one Toff in each and one Bombay had an Army PJI dispatcher.

Of Dad's stick, only two returned, Stirling amongst them. Of the 65 SAS troops that took part in Squatter, only 22 made it back after trekking through the desert on foot for 36 hours to reach their rendezvous with the LRDG. One Bombay crashed with all occupants captured. The others at least managed to exit their aircraft and jump into the storm, but some were killed on landing, being dragged and scraped along the desert floor in the gale force winds and driving rain, unable to unclip their harnesses. Others killed whilst attempting to return across the desert to the RV. The rest were captured and taken prisoner.

Whilst Paddy Maine took the losses of so many men hard, and blamed himself, Dad, laid the blame firmly at David Stirling and hated him with a passion thereafter.

David Stirling   Paddy Main

Bristol Bombay

Of the stories Dad told us as kids, I particularly remember Dad telling of a raid on an airfield. These raids (at first) were sneak in at night, lay delay action bombs and escape into the desert. Eventually the airfields got wise and guards started patrolling at night, even placing armed men in the cockpits of the stationary aircraft. This meant the raids could no longer be accomplished through stealth.

Official reports suggest airfield raids were meticulously planned. I guess many were. Dad tells it differently. One time they came across an airfield during a standard patrol. It was getting late in the evening and the men were a little merry. The plan was simply to burst in with their jeeps, drive flat out along the rows of parked aircraft and destroy them as they went. The plan was literally made on the back of a cigarette packet. The official story suggests one jeep got shot up as it raced between the rows of enemy aircraft and was abandoned mid raid. The truth of the matter is the jeep simply ran out of fuel because they had taken extra rum in the jerry cans.

Stirling subsequently decided this was a great way to fight a war and took the credit for developing the idea which now forms SAS 'official' history. I like the stories Dad told, better than official history.

Ken 'Joe' Welch (wearing the RAF PTI singlet) supervising parachute landing falls, Kabrit.

There were sad moments too as when "The Four Toffs" were asked to act as pall bearers at the funeral of SAS member Cpt Terence 'Jim' Chambers (whose parents lived at Bishops Hull in Taunton). He had returned from a long but successful SAS operation behind enemy lines in an exhausted condition. Then tragically died in December 1942 in hospital with diphtheritic infection of desert sores.

Life often reveals strange coincidence, twenty five years later, aged ten, I was swimming in the Taunton Swimming Club 50 yards Freestyle Championship and won The Chambers Trophy. It had been in Capt. Chambers family between the wars and now re engraved and donated by the family as a memorial, to the swimming club. The swimming club trophies have since been returned to the families or given permanently to the swimmer that won them on the nights they were last competed for, prior to the demolition of St James Street baths.

As the war approached its end, Dad was injured skiing whilst training in preparation for doing something covert in Yugoslavia. By the time he got back to active duty, the war was over. Dad was upset about that.

Now back in England, like many of his friends, he struggled. The Parachute Training School relocated to Upper Heyford, where it seems Dad was thrown out of married quarters for being caught in the station gym whilst in a compromising situation with a WRAF. Then during the Abingdon years, Mum and Dad had to live in a caravan. Dad left the RAF in 1954 (Mum was cross about that), returning home to Taunton where he and Mum set up a ballroom dancing school on the Parade.

Haydn Welch

Ken and Pat

Ken and Pat

Taunton School of Ballroom Dancing

14 HAYDN & LORNA

Haydn: I was delivered ten weeks premature, barely on the right side of still-born and expected to live a few hours at most. After a rushed christening, it was just a matter of time. With lungs almost too weak to breathe I had managed to last two weeks. Then a few days before Christmas there was a flu outbreak and I would certainly not survive staying in the hospital. Mum and I were sent home. Mum to avoid catching flu and me to die quietly at home, with the hope Mum might get one Christmas with her baby. Dad had other ideas and put his 'do or die' attitude to work.

Haydn with homemade bow and arrow,
Arrow approaching the top left corner.

To start with, I would cry, a lot. Dad insisted I was allowed to cry and not be comforted. When I stopped crying I would be poked and made to cry more. It was heartbreaking for Mum to hear this little baby with a feeble cry, being made to cry. But Dad had found the solution that would exercise my lungs. After all, what would any PTI think to do. I could hardly get exercise by going for a long hike across the desert. At bathtime Dad would push me under and I would hold my breath. Dad would bring me out only when the back of my neck went blue. I would take a huge lungful of air. Apparently I loved it and survived Christmas. As soon as it could be arranged, Dad had me join the Taunton Swimming Club. My earliest childhood memories are learning to swim as a baby in the St James Street small pool. I could swim a length before I could walk a length. Dad knew how to get me to live.

I spent the first seven years of my life attending a special clinic one day a week. I was taken out of school (St Andrews Infants) and always enjoyed the clinic. I would be exercised, mostly doing static exercises to encourage my lungs to develop. My favourite exercise was trying to keep a balloon in the air by blowing at it. Of course by then I was also a pretty impressive swimmer for my age and had already taken my Gold Personal Survival badge, which included distance swims in pajamas and a one mile standard swim.

Outside of school, I went feral. I liked to get up to mischief. It wasn't about the mischief, it was about the adventure, the excitement, not getting caught. Whether taking my bow and arrow to the park a short walk away from where we lived in a Council house at Horner Road, to playing on building sites, railway lines, by the river or riding my bike far too many miles away from home.

Eventually, Dad was able to buy a home of our own and aged ten, we moved to a bungalow in Eastwick Avenue. Before completing the purchase of it, Dad had already arranged to dig and plant the garden. He paid me a shilling an hour to help him and by so doing, introduced me to hard work. Much of the garden was dug and planted by the time the legal work was complete. One day I arrived home from school to find maybe twenty tons of manure outside my bedroom window. The pile was certainly five or six feet high and stretched twenty feet. It was my job to barrow it and spread it on the garden. It felt good even at that age to realise we had moved up in the world.

Denise. He loved to garden, a friend of his got him an allotment where he spent as much time as possible, he would proudly bring home his produce but my heart would sink when he arrived home with beetroot as I knew the kitchen would resemble a blood bath when he cooked them, I think it amused him that I could not wait for him to finish so I could deep clean.

Denise Welch

Haydn. Having moved out of the Council estate, didn't stop me looking for adventure with Jamie Lyndsey and Edwin Bagwell who still lived there. Breaking into schools, ransacking the tuck shop, glueing the pages of the registers together, liberating things the teachers had confiscated from the children. Setting fire to things and sometimes getting into real trouble either with them or on my own. One time with Eddy, we were up to mischief, in the car park next to St James Street swimming baths. There was this open top sports car with the keys still in the ignition, I sat in the driver's seat and removed the keys, passing them to Eddy. He proceeded to take them to the swimming baths across the road to see if they would unlock the doors, hoping we would have a swim. Whilst I opened up the glove box, a strong arm grabbed me out of the car and marched me towards Eddy, who was trying the lock of the main entrance. In an instant, Eddy grabbed his bike and took off down St James Street, towards Chapmans. I broke free and ran after him. The man gave chase Eddy, ahead of me, turned left into North Street and went flat out. I simply ran straight across the main road (without looking), into Goodlands Gardens. The man clearly saw the danger in following me, and chose to chase Eddy. He made it as far as Vivary Park before Eddy gave him the slip. An hour or so later, we met back up at Eddy's house at Lyngford Place. He still had the car keys with him. We threw them away, but kept the gonks that were on the key ring.

That summer, man landed on the moon, and we went up to separate senior schools. Eventually losing touch.

I got used to being punished. Dad would shout and bellow into my face, I knew I was in for a hiding, Then the order would come to "Fetch the stick, Jake". I knew I had to act fast and find something that Dad could beat me with. It could be a stick, a belt......anything, as long as I was quick. Whatever it was, I knew it would hurt. I knew it would go on for longer than it should. I knew

I would cry. I knew that afterwards I would have to lay on my bed until it stopped hurting.

Often a prelude to these beatings would begin a few hours sooner with being ordered to sit in the corner of the hall and just as I had sat down I would be ordered to stand in a different corner, then back again and again. All the while knowing that in five or ten minutes, or an hour, the order to get the stick would come. But when it was over, I knew it was over. One day I came home from school with a bad report. Dad decided that before we sat down for tea, I would have a beating, until I came home from school with a good report. But I didn't want to tell my teacher to write me a good report because I was being beaten at home, I chose instead to just tough it out. It took a few days before Dad gave up. Then not long after that I was in trouble again. The order came to get the stick and I thought "Stuff it", I went to my bedroom, fetched my cricket bat and shoved it in Dad's hand, with a look that said "Do your worst". I can't remember what happened next, I just know I did not get a beating. It was as if Dad thought to himself it was about time I stood up to him, lesson over, job done. I stopped being scared of him about then.

It seemed I lived in three or four camps, like Dad, and was a different person in each. A rebel with kids on the estate but OK at school. Fortunately, it was the swimming club, air cadets and church which became more influential. I became less feral, better behaved and more responsible. I would look at my church friends and realise that I wanted to be more like them than the guttersnipe I was. Or worse, the person I could become if I did not make a change. So I made the change, although in reality I had already started by giving up smoking when I was about twelve.

I reckon about this time Mum and Dad could have separated, rather than waiting another decade. Sometime around when we won the cup, Mum was maybe ready to move out and one night we were all packed up ready to go, somewhere I don't know exactly. But Mum changed her mind and we went back to bed instead. Maybe during the late 60s and 70s, divorce was often delayed for the sake of the kids, particularly as the mothers would generally be unable in those days to raise a family alone. Dad simply would not allow that.

Denise. When I was about eight years old my Mum thought it would be a good idea if I learnt to ballroom dance. She arranged for me to attend a Saturday morning class at the Pat and Ken School of Dance. I loved it from the first lesson and continued to learn and improve. Eventually I realised that I wanted to teach dance and I became a student at the school.

Naturally at some point in time Ken's path and mine crossed. I am not proud to say but we started a relationship when there was a considerable age difference between us. I was only 17 years old and Ken was 52. Ken tried to distance himself from me for many years, but that did not work and eventually we agreed to give our relationship a go, on the understanding that Ken told Pat the truth, and did not try to keep our relationship a secret.

The age difference was never a problem between us, that probably surprised many others but Ken was very young at heart and in some respects had far more "get up and go" than I. I am fully aware that the love we had for each other affected other people and their lives, thankfully Pat and Ken seemed to have a mutual respect and friendship between them. She was always kind and considerate, and would not allow anyone to put either myself or Ken down.

We married in 2002, Ken wanted a quiet wedding and we wanted my Mum's best friend to be a witness, unfortunately she was ill on the day of our wedding so Ken thought it would be a good idea to ask someone on the street to step in. Fortunately Violet's son in law arrived just in time!

The man I knew and spent a great deal of my life with was loving, affectionate, kind and he could be very funny, eccentric at times but I found that a part of his charm.

Ken's idea of parenting was quite different from my own dad's. I adored my dad and his final illness and subsequent death hit me very hard. Ken was amazing during that awful time, he made sure my mum and I ate and did his best to distract us from the grief that consumed us. It would have been almost unbearable without him. Seven years later when I lost my mum Ken was not very well himself, somehow he managed to pull it together for me and I had my husband again when I needed him most.

Thanks to our dear friend Rachel, Ken was able to be in his own home for as long as possible. She was a trusted companion which meant I could continue to work in the Dance School. It seems a kind heart and an endless supply of cheese and crackers does the trick. I loved and adored him, I still do, he was my soul mate and I miss him every day.

Denise Welch

All this while as children, Dad would take us to the beach. Often in the early evenings to avoid the crowds. He would drive his old Mini van. It had two front seats and a flat load area behind. He placed a 4 inch thick slab of foam rubber in the back upon which we would sit, lay or kneel. No such thing as seat belts in those days. When we got to the beach, if parking was tight, Dad would park parallel to the space, then stand with his back to the front of the car, picking it up under the wing and shunting it into the space. Repeating this a few times at the front and the back, until it was in place. I have no idea why, but we always helped. Dad would then take the foam rubber mattress out of the van and we would sit on it at the beach. We would visit most of the beaches nearby, Minehead, Blue Anchor, Sidmouth, Budleigh, Beer. We preferred Sidmouth as (when the tide was out) it had sand and a wonderful length of rock pools. Sadly the rock pools are now gone. Often I would swim out to a buoy with Dad. **Haydn Welch**

Let me introduce you to my youngest sister Lorna:

Lorna and Haydn

Lorna: Keeping with the theme of these writings, I also have a few anecdotal stories of my own. I am the youngest of 'Joe' Welch's children. Being female, my experiences are slightly different to those of my brother, Haydn.

It was inevitable that one day, I too would dance. That day came before I could even walk. Being born with a squint in both eyes, I was a slightly peculiar looking child. The squints became so bad I had to undergo a sight saving operation at the age of six. My sight impairment meant I was not allowed to go out on my own, I tended to fall over a lot, bump into things and had zero spatial awareness. I did not fit in well at school, with my teachers feeling I would be better off attending a 'special needs' facility nearby. As such, just before my operation, I was asked to leave, and did not return to school until I was ten years old.

My father, refused point blank to have me attend this special school, saying I would learn more if I were home schooled, something that was not really a 'thing' back in the 1960's. Home schooling, for me, meant I was placed in front of a typewriter and given history books to copy. It is fair to say I could not read or write at this point in time, although my sight was good enough to make out the shapes of letters, with the help of a magnifying glass. By the time I was ten, I was blind typing at 110 words per minute.

Another piece of equipment I was given was a sewing machine. My mother would buy clothing and fabric from bric-a-brac sales and I was given these to re-purpose. Woolen clothing were turned into pom-poms and material into all sorts of useful items. Again by the age of ten, I was making my own clothes and was very proficient at making, mending and repairing any fabric based items.

My father would have me assist him in the garden and workshop when he was home, and taught me the basics of woodworking. He would not, however, allow me near saws and other dangerous items. The one thing I could not do was get on with other children, sit still or stop chatting. I was loud, inattentive, and impulsive and generally 'too much'.

So, while my brothers were out and about doing all sorts of interesting things, I tended to be stuck at home on my own, or with either of my parents at the dancing school where I was expected to sit quietly and be on hand if they needed a dance model. Swimming was something I did once a week, because my father was adamant all of us kids must be able to swim, and swim well.

When I was eight years old, my eyesight improved considerably and I was finally allowed out on my own to go to the nearby play park. I was so excited. When I got to the park there was only one other child there, a boy younger than me. He was sat on top of those large iron rocking horses, which could hold six children. There was a bar at the back where another could push the rocking horse to get it to swing. If you pushed too hard the horse would 'bump'. Bumping the horse was not allowed and there was a large sign saying so, but of course that was the one thing all the kids wanted to do, including this other child.

 I went to the back and pushed the horse until it had enough momentum to bump. Being little, this meant I had to bend my knees to get the desired result. All was going well for a while, until I forgot to stand upright or pull back slightly on the downward swing. The horse landed on my bent legs and the boy ran off.

There I was on my own in agony, shocked and unable to stand. I do not know how long I was there, but eventually the boy who lived next door turned up and alerted my mother to the issue. The result of this accident was a longitude fracture in my right leg from my thigh to knee and knee to ankle, and I was in a plaster cast for six months, with months of physiotherapy to learn to walk again. I could no longer dance or swim and was told that I would never walk again without a limp.

Once again, my father refused to accept this and once the cast was off, my swimming became more regular and I was allowed to dance again but never fully regained my previous level of movement flow. I was slightly stiff and my footwork, while good, was not good enough to become a professional competition style dancer, which was my dream. My swimming style and coordination was shot, I was slow in comparison to my brothers and swimming became a chore not a pleasure.

My father made stilts for me to help in regaining balance and muscle strength. I was tasked to learn how to use them and we would spend hours walking around the outside of our bungalow navigating rough ground and a few steps. The height of the stilts became higher and higher until they were a good few feet off the ground. I have no doubt that had I not had those stilts the doctors may have been correct about a lifelong limp, as it was I was walking again normally within twelve months.

Haydn has already mentioned how he eventually stood up to

our father. I cannot claim that my father would punish me in the same way as he did my brothers. I guess being a girl and being 'disabled' I got off lightly. I can honestly say I have zero recollection of him ever hitting me, but I remember clearly how he was with the boys. I do recall, however, the verbal abuse and how much I hated that, wishing he would smack me and get it over with.

During my punishment sessions I had to agree with all the things he would say to me, agree that I was a bad child and agree that I deserved to be put into a care home. If I cried the punishment would continue for much longer, with my father shouting at me to be quiet, telling me that I was weak and that my emotions would kill me. I had to agree with that too.

When I was 14 years old I came home late, my mother was away, and I did not expect my father to be home so did not rush. I was wrong, he was home and I got it in a big way. He accused me of being out with 'boys' and getting up to mischief with them. This time I decided not to agree with him but did the opposite, I started to tell him exactly what I thought of him, how he was unable to keep his pants up.

My language was appalling, and I told him that I would not cower down to a piece of ...... like him and that I did not care if he hit me. I told him to come get it as I was ready, and that once he started I would not stop. I told him he would have to kill me before I stopped and all the awful things he would have to face in prison.

He response, with the biggest smile I have ever seen, was to say "That's the spunk I am looking for, now go to bed, you have school in the morning."

The following day, I beat up the girl who had been bullying me at school, and I did not stop the attack when the teachers came to split us up, hitting them too. I was excluded for a week and my father collected me from school. He was so pleased with me he bought me an ice-cream. From that day onwards my father never had a go at me again and I became a 'Good'un'.

The bullying stopped too, and I made it very clear that if anyone said, or did, anything 'not nice' to me again I would hurt them. While I was also going to church with my brother, I cannot say that I became the model citizen. The truth is I started to live a double life. I would drink, take drugs and smoke when out with my non church friends, and a goody two shoes with my church friends. I got myself into all sorts of trouble most of which I managed to get away with.

As for my relationship with my father, well that just started to get better and better, or stranger and stranger may be a more appropriate way of explaining it.

I was 16 when I got caught for shoplifting. When my father found out, he was not at all angry that I had stolen something, he was upset that I had been caught. He then went on to explain how I could do the same thing and get away with it, on the understanding that steeling was only acceptable when you had no other choice, and when it would not harm anyone else. Over the years, he also taught me the rights and wrongs with regards to lying. If for any reason you cannot tell the truth, the story you make up needs only to put an element of doubt into someone else's mind and that there is a possibility that your words are true. Most of all that once a story has been told you must never admit that it was not true and keep that story for the rest of your life. If you cannot do that, say nothing at all. I look back now and realised that from my father's point of view the war was never over. He always expected that at some point we would have to face it, and when that time came his teachings would keep us alive.

Being socially excluded, I spent hours at the dancing school during the day and night. I loved the music and watching my parents work. By the time I was fourteen I was teaching both adults and children and started giving private lessons at the age of sixteen. It appeared at that time my future was to be a dance teacher. When it came to dance partners, I had a choice of Mum or Dad. While I preferred my mum as my Ballroom partner for her graceful movements, my father was the go-to for Latin. When it came to the energy and rhythm of jives, cha-cha, sambas, and rumbas, he was unmatched.

When I was seventeen I was, a bit on the chubby side. I'd always dreamed of learning the classic 'airplane lift' move, like the one made famous years later in Dirty Dancing. Although the movie wasn't out for another ten years, I had the same idea: that soaring, exhilarating lift.

One day, I mentioned it to my father. We were in our small kitchen with a ceiling no higher than eight feet, if that. He looked at me and simply said, "Come on, then—let's try it." I hesitated, unsure of how to start. But he reassured me, saying, "Just run up, put your arms out, and jump. I'll do the rest. All you have to do is trust me, arch your back and stay still."

So I did. I ran toward him, arms open, and he lifted me effortlessly, it seemed. Despite the low ceiling and my extra weight, he held me there, suspended in mid-air. He kept his arms slightly bent to avoid the ceiling. For a full ten seconds, he held me steady, letting me savour the moment. Then, with complete control, he guided me down, took my hands, and slid me smoothly between his legs, back to a standing position.

It was exhilarating and unforgettable. To this day, I've never attempted that move with anyone else. That dance, that moment, belonged to just the two of us. I am smiling remembering that day.

But, like Haydn has mentioned, "There are some things you do when at the time you are doing them, you don't realise it will be the last time you will ever do that thing". That time for me came when I was twenty one. I was teaching an older man to dance in a private lesson, when he became far too friendly. Suffice to say I never danced again, nor did I tell anyone the reason why.

The 'airplane lift'. Dirty Dancing.

Much earlier, when we were still kids, I recall Haydn getting stung by a hornet when he sat on it while we were at the beach in

Sidmouth. Immediately realising what had happened, with my brother showing signs of toxic shock, my father lifted him up, stripped off his swimming trunks, and simultaneously started to suck the poison out of his buttock while running towards the first aid centre which was not at all close. Can you image the scene, a completely naked youth with his bottom being sucked by an elderly man, running at an incredible high speed up the beach, with two other kids trying and failing miserably to catch up.

Another time, while I was out with Haydn, and wanting change to put into the Kit Kat vending machine (I was about ten at the time) I impulsively ran across the road to see if the people on the other side had change. I did not stop to look if the road was clear, it wasn't! I was hit by a car, landed on top of the bonnet and when the car came to an emergency stop, I was thrown forwards onto the road with my legs straight out in front of me in an upright sitting position, until I finally came to a stop. My bother ran home to alert my father, who turned up at the same time as the ambulance. There was no room for him to come with me in the ambulance to the hospital, which was two miles away. Taking into account that this was a blue light trip, somehow my father who had run to the hospital, arrived there before we did. Haydn remembers the incident, having been looking into a shop window and on hearing the bang, he looked up and saw me through the reflection of the shop window, flying through the air.

A story my mother once told me, also related to the speed in which my father acted. They were still at Abingdon and living in a caravan on a caravan site. It was late at night and my mother was getting into her nightie for bed. All the lights were on, and there were a whole group of holiday makers having a noisy get together outside one of the neighbouring vans. With that, my mother noticed an extremely large insect inside her nightie and began to scream, in an instant Dad had stripped the nightie off her, leaving her completely naked and visible to this group, and threw it out of the door. He then started to jump on the said garment to kill whatever was inside it. When he realised he and Mum were being watched, he turned to the group and said in a very firm voice "Is that good enough entertainment for you, now be quiet and go to bed, I have to get up in the morning" turned around and went back into the van. They heard no more from this group, not a squeak.

Lorna also remembered:

And then there was the goat, who decided to jump in front of our Mini while on the way to the beach. Thinking the goat was dead, my father picked it up and put it in the van. When we got out of the car he realised the goat was not dead, so we took it to the beach with us, and home again. We did plead with him to let us keep it, but that was not to be and we were told he had given it to the RSPCA. I have no idea if that was true, or the goat became dinner.

My father had a soft spot for animals. One of our cats, called Poddy, was found by him and brought home, and the next cat Smokey, was found in a dustbin at the dancing studio (possibly left behind by a pupil, knowing Dad would bring it home to the children). A few weeks later Smokey had kittens, but only Toby survived. We were then a three cat household. We also had a German Shepherd, who was not exercised as regularly as she should have been, but would always accompany us to Smeatharpe Airfield, where Tan would be dropped off while myself and my brothers would be allowed to drive the car, with Tan chasing us behind.

Lorna Welch

Haydn, Goat, Lorna, Mark, Dad on foam rubber mattress.

On the subject of cats, Denise had this to say referring to their holidays in Greece.

Ken always wanted to feed the stray cats on holiday, he would buy food and even though I would warn him about getting too attached it fell on deaf ears. Going back to the airport was a nightmare as he would worry about who would feed them now. On arriving home to our own cat I would be told that I was spoiling her and that she would never appreciate how lucky she was, yes, she was lucky.

Ken loved animals. On our first Christmas together I wanted to buy him an Alsatian puppy. I asked Pat for her advice, she very wisely reminded me of the work involved and that she was sure he would be pleased but to consider how busy we both were and to think carefully. I took her advice. That Christmas however he surprised me with a kitten, he had already chosen her name (Jessica) and brought her home on Christmas Eve. We both adored her of course. Ken never missed a vet appointment whether serious or not with any of our pets and he never hid his distress when the time to say goodbye came. I think that is the sign of a real man. In 2003 he bought me two kittens, a boy and a girl, we named the boy 'Joe' because of Ken's nickname in the RAF, those cats were a great comfort to me in the years to come.

Denise Welch

Haydn: Summer holidays were always spent with Mum at Nana's in Swanage, and days spent mostly at Buck Shore beach in front of the Grosvenor Hotel (now a water works) with the old pier to the left. Dad would only ever stay one day before returning to run the dancing schools. It never occurred to me until I was married myself, that actually, Dad was taking his own holiday elsewhere, with Denise. It seems Dad lived in two camps, all kept secret from the children. I simply had no idea. Looking back, it was clear Denise was the love of his life. Our home was simply a place where Dad lived. There was no romance with Mum. Dad's heart lived elsewhere. Really, he should have married Denise much sooner.

In that day we spent on holiday with him, he encouraged us to earn holiday money. He gave us one penny each if we clambered up onto the pier and jump off. Sixpence if we swam around the pier with him. I would often climb on his back to have a rest during the swim. One day aged about 5 ¼, he sent me around the pier on my own. It was not so much the distance, but being alone. I remember being quite frightened swimming past the far end, in the sea, looking into the foreboding shadowy structure of gribble infested oak timbers. Not that I knew they were gribble infested or oak back then. All I knew was they looked very scratchy and frightening. I gave the pier a wide birth not wanting the waves to push me into it. Dad gave me a shilling. Dad liked this beach and we rarely went to any of the others along the seafront. He even taught my oldest sister Juliet to swim in the sea there. The pier in the late 1940s was quite different then. Even a decade and two later when I played there, it was still complete with sun decks and diving boards (even though it was already abandoned) with much of it having fallen into the sea. Nowadays, there remains just a few stumps to give a clue of what once proudly withstood Hitler's storm.

Ken and Juliet 1948

It was on these holidays that I would stare out to sea at the Isle of Wight, and thinking it was France, I promised Mum I would swim there one day. Funny thing is, when you look at it from Swanage, mainland to mainland, looks so close compared to France but is actually about the same distance as the English Channel if you exclude The Needles. When I realised it was not actually France, I was quite disappointed. I no longer wanted to swim to France, I wanted to swim to the Isle of Wight instead. It had become iconic to me. Now probably sixty years later, and having swam to France twice already I kind of think that maybe I might just do this swim from Swanage to the Isle of Wight...... one day.

It was whilst I was standing at the foot of the new pierj I bumped into Mervyn Sharp. I had no idea who he was apart from he was the 'King of the Channel', having swam it seven times. He was doing a training swim from Swanage to Bournemouth. I asked him for his autograph and had my picture taken with him. I was fourteen or fifteen and had just won the 400 yard freestyle representing Somerset County. I was that close to asking if I could swim alongside him for some of the way. But I didn't. I just watched him swim off. That was a life changing moment, lost.

Every year at Swanage I would always swim around the pier, often multiple times. As I got older I would swim across the bay until the beach ran out and I hit the cliffs. The first time I did that swim, I knew it was too far, but I did it anyway. Scrambling ashore I decided to walk back. I can't remember when I first wanted to do extreme things, but even as a young child, I was always up for the adventure. It didn't matter whether anyone was there to watch out for me, I just did what I wanted, as long as it frightened me a little.

I was always inspired by Dad's stories and simply wanted to make a few of my own. Whether climbing too high in a tree, or cycling too far and getting lost, clambering along Swanage pier until the timbers ran out, and always swimming, sometimes straight out to sea until I got scared and turned back for shore. Swimming the English Channel was always going to happen. Dad had already laid that foundation.

It was Al Alvarez, a writer and mountaineer in Chris Bonnington's era who said it best, writing of his friend Mo Anthoine who related the need to climb as a need to 'feed the rat'. It was as if a rat were gnawing away at your bones, constantly chewing. The rat needed the adventure, he needed to be fed and would chew away at your bones until you relented and provided the adventure it craved. If you fed the rat with hills to climb, it would be satisfied for a while. You would get home and the gnawing would have stopped. Then in a while the rat returned for more, demanding another adventure. You relent and give it the

Alps. Then, after returning home again, you become aware once more of the chewing away in your bones. Constant chewing, chewing and chewing. It never really stops, until you provide more adventure. You give it the Himalayas and the rat is satisfied for another season. Alvarez wrote, "That's why I like feeding the rat. It's a sort of annual check-up on myself. The rat is you, really. It's the other you, and it's being fed by the you, you think you really are". His climbing partner Mo Anthoine had this to say, "To snuff it without knowing who you are and what you are capable of, I can't think of anything sadder than that." And the Rat? The rat is that other climber inside you, the one that thinks you're spectacularly adventurous and skillful. "When they come close to each other, that's smashing, that is."

   I imagine sometimes Nicola would prefer to hit that rat with a spade, but even now, it chews away at my bones seeking the next adventure. I keep telling the rat that my dreams must never become the stuff of her nightmares. There are so many things I haven't done because of that thought and the rat keeps on chewing.

   I can't remember when we stopped going to Swanage as a family but when I was older I went on my own and spent the week with Uncle Bob on the pier with Divers Down. Uncle Bob taught me to Scuba.

Denise tells a couple of holiday stories with Dad.

We both loved to holiday on the Greek islands, both loving the sun and beach life, Corfu was a favourite and on arriving the first thing Ken wanted to do was to hire a motorbike, we travelled miles, me on the back of course. Very little clothes were worn, no helmet as health and safety didn't figure big in those days. The only time we had a slight incident, involved Ken cutting his arm quite badly and a local vet came to the rescue, he cleaned the wound arranged antibiotics and visited the next day to check on him. What surprised us most was the fact there actually was a vet on the island! Those holidays together are precious memories, maybe too much food and wine were consumed but life is for living. About 1997 Ken decided he wanted to learn to speak Greek, he went to evening class and did extremely well, he did his homework and was about to take his first exam but the Dance School got really busy about then and unfortunately he just didn't have the time to continue.

Denise Welch

Denise and Ken

In the daytime Dad would work as a labourer. He actually stole the timber from the building site to build me a cot. In the evenings he would teach dancing at the Taunton studio. Eventually Dad opened a second studio in Bridgwater. Often he would run the ten miles to and from Bridgwater to teach at the studio, whilst Mum taught in Taunton. When I was older he encouraged me to run with him. Looking back now, I wish I had joined him, but I never did. I regret not running with him.

Due to Mum and Dad teaching at the dancing schools, for me the Taunton Swimming Club was a great baby sitter. Often armed with sixpence for the bus ride home or sometimes Eric Copp would give me a sixpence. I would buy chips from the chip shop in St James Street, and walk the one mile home instead. Other times I caught the bus, although I actually missed the bus more often than not. I tended not to wait at the bus stop on the Bridge, I waited at the far end of the Bridge because there was a Jaguar dealership there. I would stare into their window particularly at a primrose open top E Type. It was £1795 and I started saving my bus fare to buy it. Often I would not notice the bus arriving as my head was cupped in my hands as I peered through the window. I would miss the bus anyway, walk home and save my sixpence.

I only remember Dad watching me race once. Having won the Chambers Trophy a few months earlier, Dad took me to Bath to compete in the Somerset County Age Group Championships. I entered the 11 and under 100 yards freestyle. I swam the heats quite normally and won a place in the final albeit in 6th place. It seemed this was another race I would not win, except this time Dad would see me fail. However, something special happened in the final, I found a way to swim my heart out to win the race. I was the Somerset County Champion and Dad saw me do it.

The Chambers and Howe trophies.

It was 1968 and the year of the Mexico Olympics. Taunton Swimming Club (and Great Britain) were represented by David Hembrow, who sadly returned having missed out on a medal after finishing 4th in the men's 4 x 100m freestyle relay. Nevertheless he received a hero's welcome home. Whilst home he entered the

179

swimming club 100 yards freestyle championship. For him a demonstration swim. It seemed the whole town wanted to watch him race. The balcony was heaving with spectators. I would always enter every race I could, so aged 11, I too entered the men's race (after all I was the Somerset Age Group Champion for 11 and under). Again swimming my heart out in the heats aiming only for a personal best time. Then settled down to watch the senior swimmers swim their heats. All eyes on our Olympic hero. Unbeknown to me, the senior swimmers had all agreed that David was going to win and so they concocted an ad hoc plan that for the heats, they would all do a belly flop dive and start the first length as if they were non swimmers. They would then race three lengths to try to win their places in the final. It was extraordinary to watch. To my total surprise, my best time in the heats gave me 5th place in the final. I was going to swim a championship race next to an Olympian.

There I was trying my best to be five feet tall, standing on a diving block in lane one, next to five other swimmers. One an Olympian, another Alan Wheeler was a National Schoolboys champion for 100m freestyle and three others, probably Dave Thorp, Chris Thorp and Gerry Ballantyne all of whom were so tall their heads were at cloud base.

Mum was above me in the balcony cheering, along with everybody else. The Starting Marshall blew his whistle and the everything fell silent. "Take your Marks", I crouched on the starting block. The gun went off. The noise of cheering was immediate and immense, even before I hit the water, it was all I could hear. I don't remember much of the swim, apart from the cheering. I had competed many times, but this time I could feel the noise. How many times can a swimmer swim his heart out in one night? I can tell you, at least twice. The cheering got louder and louder, it was fantastic. Then what seemed like all of a sudden, it stopped, just as I approached my tumble turn at the end of the third length. The race was over and I felt awkward, I was that far behind and still had one length to swim. Then the magic started, realising there was still a swimmer in, the cheering resumed and I tell you, this time it was louder still. The whole balcony of spectators were cheering, and it was all for me.

I came last by a length. It was the best race of my life. I knew then I wanted to swim for England. I knew then I would one day stand on other podiums, wear medals around my neck and wave the Union Jack above my head. I knew one day I would swim the English Channel.

Reflecting on that race now, the truth of the matter occurs to me that I was robbed. I should have won that trophy that day. All the senior swimmers should have been disqualified due to their humour violation (if such a rule existed back then). Funny though, having spoken with one of them to see how it all happened from their point of view, he had no recollection of it.

Sometime around then, the senior swimmers attended a training camp at Crystal Palace where they had swam one mile butterfly as a warm up. On their return to Taunton, they made me do it and the baths manager gave me a one year season ticket for succeeding.

I swam that race every year for four more years before I won that trophy.

Same boy, same table, different trophies.

If I remember right (after all, was fifty years ago) the trophy was called The Chivers Trophy. A sterling silver round bowl with handles and a black plinth. Looking down the engraved list of previous winners, there was David Hembrow 1968. Another name caught my eye, W James 1956. It couldn't be, could it? I took the trophy to school to show my PE teacher. I had raced him once in the school swimming sports when I was eleven and beat him by a touch. (I actually chose to attend Ladymead School because my older brother went to Priorswood, and I refused to go through school as his little brother). The clincher of course was that Ladymead had its own swimming pool. It was the perfect school for me. My PE teacher wouldn't race me again after that swim when I was in the first year. I approached him, now in the fourth or fifth year, holding up the trophy. From across the room I saw him smile. I knew at that moment, my PE teacher Bill James was the one engraved on the trophy as a previous winner.

During these early teenage years at the swimming club, myself, Anthony Donnan, Robert Stone and Graham Bandey were getting pretty good at our individual strokes. I would swim freestyle, Tony was a butterfly swimmer, Bob was backstroke and Graham swam breaststroke. Then one day around 1970, Graham's dad had a heart attack whilst swimming, and died. With our new found teenage independence, we would cycle around to Graham's house to provide him with company, we were no longer just team mates, we began to become close friends.

These friendships rapidly replaced those with my old friends. These were a good set of lads. At thirteen years old I became fond of Graham's sister who was eleven. We were childhood sweethearts for two years. Over the next three or four years, our weekends and summers would often be spent together, looking for adventure without mischief. We spent time listening to LPs. I tended not to have any, but Electric Warrior, Led Zeppelin 2 and Deep Purple In Rock were favourites.

We cycled the ten miles to Bridgwater Lido and decided that rather than get out when it was time to cycle home, we would get thrown out instead. To do this we had to get to the diving boards and perform the most outrageous jumps and dives. Often we would get two or three great (dangerous) dives in before the whistle blew and we were thrown out.

After Wednesday night club training sessions, we would wait for the pool to empty and the adults to disappear, we would then jump off the balcony. Shared experiences, the adversity of tough swimming sessions and good friendships created a strong bond both in and out of the pool.

One year, now aged 16, the Somerset Age Group Championships were being held in Taunton. Having been a former 11 and under County freestyle champion, I was now competing to be the 16 and under freestyle champion. Teams from all over the County arrived at the pool in St James Street. One team in particular always caught the swimmers attention. Millfield. The most expensive public school in the Country arrived and sat themselves down together in a corner. We watched them carefully. They always had a strong team and always wanted (even expected) to get first, second and third in every race.

But this was my pool, my town, and I was determined they would not make a clean sweep in my race. So I swam my best for my hundred, and as expected Millfield swimmers did very well. I can't remember who came first or second, but I came third and spoilt their day. I also remember the boy that came fourth, a very striking, tall, bald headed lad by the name of Duncan Goodhew.

Of course, about this time, I left school and got a job for £30 a week. Duncan stayed on at Millfield, went to university and kept training, eventually getting gold at the Moscow Olympics in 1980.

Streaking had become a thing. One evening we agreed to do a 'streak'. Once the pool was cleared, we sneaked up to the balcony. When carefully standing on the top tier bench seats we could reach the cast iron girder that spanned the width of the pool. We would go hand over hand, high above the pool, dangling beneath this girder. Gradually getting higher and higher and further out from the balcony. At the highest point, the cast iron was much thinner and it wobbled as we travelled along it. The idea was, once at the highest point (over the deep end and facing the main entrance towards the shallow end), we would let go with one hand, untie our Speedos and wriggle out of them. We were not allowed to completely let go of the girder until our trunks hit the water. Then we would drop thirty feet into the pool. The strange thing was, nobody ever caught us doing it, so really, as far as streaking was concerned, it probably didn't count.

Then back into the changing room, which for a while was at the far end of the pool near the stairwell for the balcony. We liked that changing room the most. It had water pipes, which passed through the walls at ceiling height of the ten foot square room. Often we were the only boys using it and (if others were also using it, we would get dressed slowly until we had it to ourselves). It didn't take us long to figure out that (one at a time) we could hold onto one of the overhead pipes and do a chin up with it. Then with our face pressed against the side of the pipe, we could peer through a one inch gap in the wall, through which the pipe ran. The other side of the wall, was the girls changing room. Sometimes we got lucky, until our arms gave out, and another boy took his chance.

Summer times found us attending swimming training camps at Barton Hall in Torquay, or Sand Bay near Brean where Graham and I made a couple more efforts to streak, but still we made sure the coast was clear before we ran. Then back home, we decided to go all in. We were at a disco at Staplegrove Village Hall, the dance floor was heaving. We would sneak behind the stage, get undressed and run the length of the dance floor, out the main doors around to the back door and get our clothes. My heart was racing. There were so many people and we would not be shy. Then, suddenly, there was a commotion between records, the crowd on the dance floor parted and two bigger boys ran straight past us, completely naked. We lost our nerve, we couldn't compete.

Twenty or so years later, the four of us got back together. I had challenged the current Taunton Swimming Club to invite us to compete against them in a 4x50 medley relay. Our 1975 squad against their current 1995 squad. Bob swam his 50 backstroke and had lost a yard or so, Graham took over with his breaststroke and lost another. Tony was fantastic, his butterfly was far faster than theirs and he gave me a lead for bringing it home front crawl.

Well, I always said you had to learn to lose before you learn to win. I was overhauled, and their teenage squad, beat us forty year olds. In the pub afterwards, things were different, only Graham was drinking. I reminded my team mates how I was mildly mocked for giving up drinking in my mid-teens, after having become a member of The Church of Jesus Christ of Latter-day Saints, and now they had all stopped drinking too.

Sadly, my swimming club friends and I lost touch again after that 40 year reunion race. We all went back to making a living and another twenty five years passed us by.

Recently, I spent some time trying to locate them. Now as OAPs, I had the idea to reform the medley relay team, and swim the English Channel again, this time being a World First Medley Relay. It didn't happen. Although I managed to find Bob Stone, and phoned him. After the expected swear words, the next thing he said was "No, I won't be swimming the English Channel with you". I still haven't found Tony Donnan, but sadly Graham Bandey (now Cartwright) died some months later.

Looking back at these guys, the example and outlook they had, (compared to my earlier friends) and the opportunities that swimming presented to me, I knew I had something I loved and was good at, I had found a better way. At around this same time having also made new friends at church, I realised that these were the kind of people that I wanted to become. Somewhere during these early teenage years I changed from being a street urchin and guttersnipe to a young man looking forward to a life of adventure. A life where Dad, having inspired the earliest dreams I had as a seven year old, of being an astronaut, climbing Everest, swimming for England and hiking to the South Pole in the footsteps of Scott, were never wasted. I found a proper way to seek the adventure and excitement I craved. Hope became my favourite word.

Over the following years, I threw myself into doing some pretty exciting things from nearly drowning whilst trying to freedive sump three at Swildon's Hole, getting stuck after 45 seconds in the tight spot near the exit of the submerged tunnel and choosing to return to the entrance rather than carry on. I was underwater for nearly two minutes. To rock climbing in the Avon Gorge and falling off twice (thankfully my fall being arrested by my climbing partner clamping on the rope as it spun through his carabiners). Maintaining the hope that one day I would still climb Everest, do the South Pole and the other things.

Many of these adventures were without any training. If I went caving, it was often on my own. Hiking in the hills with no equipment and sleeping under a hedge. Where training was required, like parachuting, Dad always thought the training was too recreational. He didn't like the relaxed undisciplined approach at Dunkeswell. Hang gliding in the 70s in the hills around Meare was conducted by a group of former hippies (I didn't tell Dad that bit). Paragliding was in it's infancy, but was more controlled and at least had a training syllabus. By the time paramotors were developed a couple decades later, such training was properly regulated. Flying would become the arena for most adventures. But actually it was never about the adrenaline, but the freedom.

Although the cost involved, especially for a full pilots license. was too great when raising a family, I eventually stopped and stuck with Microlights. I realized then that I couldn't justify the cost of some things both in terms of money and ultimately where it might lead. For instance, an hours training in a Cessna was once £100 compared to a holiday for two weeks in Spain costing £200. Many adventures went unfulfilled so they would not become a new mistress. I asked my boss if I could take a whole year's holiday entitlement, back to back. Being clever with the dates, bank holidays and weekends, it would give me four weeks. And if it took longer, I would risk the telling off, even dismissal. He wanted to know why. I explained, so I could hike Kathmandu to base camp. He said no. It was that moment that I knew for certain, I would start my own business and make my own permissions.

Haydn (aged 17) flying at Mere with a Rogallo hang glider

One thing about Dad which was very special. He knew how to work, and work hard. Labouring in the days and teaching at nights. Work had value. So, coming from a family which recognised the importance of work, particularly being self-employed, gave me an edge. Getting a job and working for someone else always seemed second best, compared with working for yourself. Being my own boss was always on the cards.

I was however torn, from wanting to join the RAF and follow in Dad's footsteps to fly or jump. Join the Marines as a swimmer/canoeist or take a couple years out, and serve as a missionary. All of these things were boiling away.

   I wasn't quite ready to become a missionary, although it got very close as one by one I saw my closest friends at church, become missionaries for two years.

   I had already been accepted into the RAF but, like Dad, did not get the position I wanted. Walking into their careers office, I sat down with the recruiting staff and said I wanted to join the air force as a Physical Training Instructor. I spent the next twenty minutes telling them why. They loved the swimming stories and were pleased with my ATC service and how I was able to get myself in the air the only way I could. Having County standard status in swimming was vital. I had no idea, but in those days, to become a PTI, RAF selection demanded County standard status in two sports and I only had it in one. I was offered a position as a Weapons Mechanic. I was gob smacked. But signed up anyway and went home quite disappointed.

   The time came for basic training. I handed in my notice where I worked in the Unemployment Benefit Office and was to catch the train on Monday morning. I went to the barbers and had a crew cut, packed my suitcase and was ready to go, but something was wrong. I realised the last thing I wanted to do for the next twelve years was maintain weapons and that if I started training, I would love the training and camaraderie, but hate my job.

   I made an instant life changing decision. With my packed case, new haircut and every penny I had in my pocket. I got on the train (a day early), then took a ferry across the Channel. I was in Holland at the time I was due to take the Queen's shilling. Maybe I just needed a few months to sort things out, and become a missionary

   I felt 'called' and just needed to prepare properly. The RAF would have to wait a couple of years. I stayed in Holland until my money ran out. The timing of that day, the day I was down to my last £15 and the consequences that would unfold would bring the most life changing moment I would experience. Looking back I see the hand of God, He still loved me even if He couldn't use me as a missionary.

When my money ran out, I returned to England, the plan was to stay with Big John at his flat in Bristol. We would prepare to be missionaries together. The next day, walking down the street with John, past the job centre, I noticed a vacancy for a shop assistant in a High Street Jewellers. I popped in to enquire about it, and was asked if I could attend an interview that afternoon. With my £15, I went into Hepworth's and bought a new suit. Had the interview and was offered the job there and then, I would start on Monday. That evening, the area manager phoned me and asked if I would work in their Exeter branch instead of Bristol. I agreed. I became a retail jeweller and Big John later spent two years as a missionary.

I maintain to this day, the only reason I did not become an astronaut, climb Everest or become a missionary was simply because I did not do the required things that placed me, or kept me on those paths. But the childhood dream to become an astronaut, was not in vain. Dreams are never wasted.

Haydn

I took up lodgings with a church family in Exeter, with the intention to prepare to be a missionary and started my new job as the assistant manager for Ratner's Jewellers. I loved it. There was a thrill helping people choose an item and then taking the money. There was a different thrill when helping a couple choose an engagement ring and sharing an insight into something special. There were growing up moments too. I remember selling a wedding ring to a guy, he had come in with a mate. He chose his ring and then (surprisingly to me), he asked his mate which one he liked. They then chose his ring together. Of course, they were not allowed to get married, but were planning their own version. I had never knowingly met a gay person before. Now, here were two men buying rings for each other. The look they had in their eyes, the feelings I saw passing between them and the things they said, were just as lovely as 'normal' couples. Taking their payment behind the scenes, I whispered to the manger that I was serving a gay couple with wedding rings, was it allowed? He wanted to walk across the shop to take a look at them. It was 1977.

Nicola had the most beautiful smile. A total joy.

After a few months, we needed a new sales assistant. I would meet and greet, the manager would interview. A few people came for the interviews and at the end of the day, the manager had made his choice. I was disappointed, the lady he chose had been a little aloof. I asked why he hadn't chosen one of the others, in particular one who had a lovely smile, bright eyes and was immediately a person a customer could feel at ease with and with whom I had talked briefly. It seemed the lady he chose was more experienced. I said it was the wrong choice. Well, the lady was offered the job, but she turned it down and I got my choice after all.

Another few months passed, and this new girl had an idea to invite me to church. She had brought a Book of Mormon to work, and was going to give it to me, but she 'chickened out'. She had no idea I was planning to be a missionary, and here she was hoping to invite me to a church I was already attending, even though she was not a member. Some missionary I was going to make, when I should have been the one inviting her.

A week or two later she was invited to a party but she needed a lift to get there. She asked if I would drive her. So I did. At the party she kissed me. It was lovely.

It was only a few weeks later that I handed in my notice, in order to work for a competitor across the road, so I could afford flying lessons. Instead my area manage doubled my salary and I was transferred to Cambridge, a six hour drive in my old Austin A 35. It was time for another life changing moment.

Nicola and I stayed up ages trying to figure out what to do. I loved being at work with her, and now that was over, just because I wanted to fly and the job was going to enable me to do so. The solution was so simple, but nevertheless took a couple of hours to pop into my mind. I simply said, "Come too".

Nicola came to Cambridge with me, it was the best decision we ever made. She immediately got a job in another jewellers just two doors away. One day, she popped in to say a ring had arrived in stock that she really liked, and did I think she should buy it. I remarked that she had a good staff discount and didn't need me to decide for her, just buy it if she liked it. She thought that I should see it first and I should go in over my lunch break and take a look.

How I missed the signs, I don't know, but it was always going to happen. Her lovely smile and happy positive countenance has made life a real joy. Thank goodness I ran out of money when I did. If I had £20 more in my pocket and returned from Holland a couple days later, I would never have found her. Nicola is a dream come true and it happened, all because my money ran out.

Family has been life's greatest adventure and our two boys came along to join in.

Joe & Ben

We had moved to Eastbourne, to manage a brand new jewellery shop in the Arndale Centre. One day a customer came in wanting to buy a silver initial. The shop did not sell them and head office would not help. I didn't want to say no to a customer for such a simple thing. I phoned a supplier I had a relationship with during an earlier job and had to buy a whole alphabet of initials just to get the one my customer needed. She bought the initial and I put the money in my pocket. I then took my pack of initials home and in the evening went door to door where I lived.

After ninety minutes walking around the block, knocking on doors, I returned home with more money in my pocket than I earnt in a day. In the end, I bought a few more items that the shop did not sell. When a customer would come in, I showed them a small collection of what I had, made a sale and kept the money. After a few weeks, I had built up a range of similar things. Instead of keeping them in a box under the counter, I made up a small display and put them in the window. A few things would sell every now and again. Some evenings I would again go door to door.

One lady at the door asked if I did parties like Tupperware. I didn't but said that I did. She booked me for a jewellery party. It didn't take long before I was doing jewellery parties across Eastbourne. I still had my silver initials at the shop in the window.

One day, the area manager turned up unannounced. I rushed to hide the small display I had in the window, while he parked the car. I knew then that selling my few items in the shop was taking the mickey but I also knew then that what I had started was just the beginning. I would soon hand in my notice, return to Taunton and Nicola and I would start our own business.

I remembered the time I had my first bike, the places I would go, the things I would do. I remembered these dreams when giving our two boys their first bikes for Christmas and seeing their excitement. I could see in them, their enthusiasms and the places they would go on their bikes. I sat down that Christmas and made a list of the hopes and dreams I had at their age. An age when it didn't matter what the dream was, they would all come true when I was older. I realised I was now older and many (most) of my dreams remained to be done. The first items on my list of 'Things to do before I die" was to be an astronaut, climb Everest and walk to the South Pole. Somewhere around item eight, I wrote swim the English Channel.

Haydn: English Channel, 17hrs 2mins World's first Backstroke. 1993.

I first swam the Channel in 1992 and fulfilled the childhood dream, but the rat was not satisfied. On the way home, my coach Tom Watch suggested for the next year I swim to France and back, a two way nonstop swim. I immediately said no. He then suggested I do another single crossing instead, but swim backstroke. I asked him why backstroke. He replied "Because it hasn't been done before". I spent two or three seconds thinking about it and said "Yes". I still don't know which of these two swims I enjoyed best, the childhood dream or the World first.

Those years training for and swimming the Channel were special but I struggled to maintain my mojo. The training was too tough, I needed a break and try something more recreational. I had heard of an Italian guy who was freediving. Diving as deep as he could on a single breath of air. I quite fancied the idea and booked a course in Plymouth with Howard Jones. I believe it was the first course in the UK. The course was fun but nothing more than an introduction, more like extreme snorkeling.

Freediving in the UK was in it's infancy. I looked further afield and found Aharon and MT Solomans teaching in Paxos. This was more like it. I spent a week learning to dive deep. Returned to England and started to mix it with maybe twenty others actively freediving in England. We booked a couple of trips to Dahab, freediving the Blue Hole and generally teaching ourselves by trial and error and returning to Paxos a couple of times. Howard organized annual competitions in Cyprus and created a buzz that energised many European freedivers. A good few were accomplishing depths a little short of 100 meters. A freedive buddy Marcus Greatwood and I were invited to Tomsk in Siberia to spend a month fin swimming with their junior team. The thought being to see how sprint finning with a monofin could be adapted to slow finning for greater depth. Monofins were quite a revelation at that time and very few were in the UK.

Whilst I loved the recreational nature of the sport, I really enjoyed competing. Freediving had two disciplines both undertaken by holding your breath. 'Constant Weight' is a standard dive as deep as you could go, in the sea, using fins, and 'Static Apnea' a simple timed event, to find who could hold their breath the longest, laying face down in the pool. A new discipline was beginning to emerge, 'Dynamic Apnea', an event swam in a pool to find the person who could swim the greatest underwater distance, either with or without fins.

I enjoyed dynamic apnea, it was an event I could train for in a pool, so I started to train. At this time, most freedivers were just people that liked the idea of freediving. Nobody was really training. They went on courses and dive trips but that was pretty much it. None were athletes. Whilst they played, I trained daily. After a few months I travelled to Switzerland to compete and swam 125 meters, a few weeks later I competed again, in France and reached 139 meters. This swim created a new British record. In 2002, the British Freediving association selected a team to represent the UK. I was selected to swim the Dynamic Apnea event. I was going to 'swim' for England in Hawaii.

The whole Hawaii experience was simply the best. For my swim, fairly early in the competition, I swam 156 meters but was disqualified, the judges considered that when I surfaced, I was too close to being unconscious. My event was over. Quite disappointed, I sat to watch the remaining competitors. The world record holder Herbert Nitsch swam 144 meters and Pierre Frolla swam 150 meters to win the event.

Around this time I was having trouble with my heart behaving erratically. As freediving was so new, doctors had little idea of the effect that breath holding and depth, might have on certain conditions. I had to stop freediving. My British Record stood for about two years, about the same time it took to fix my heart. However, due to a complication during surgery, my Phrenic nerve was damaged resulting in partial paralysis of my diaphragm. I could still breath unaided but only passively.

Returning from hospital I went for a gentle swim in the sea with a friend who had two young children, they came with us. When they got tired, they would climb on our backs for a rest. During this time, I was completely unable to get sufficient oxygen and had to ensure my friend took care of both children. I simply could not do anything but lay on my back and breathe. Getting ashore and recovering, it bothered me that I could not even swim 200 yards.

I popped into a beach shop and bought a boogie board and a pair of cheap fins, then while my friend swam, I lay on the board and gently kicked. It was perfect and I felt I could do it all day. I had booked a couple weeks freediving in Egypt with a few buddies, but still went along, even though it was doubtful if I would do any deep freedives. The nerve damage was rapidly repairing and my breathing beginning to normalize and I considered it was time to start being more active. I had bought a small inflatable 'raft' that I could lay on and kick with fins. The raft would also hold a water bottle, camera and a few bits and pieces. I would use the week to start swimming.

We took a boat ride to a reef about ten miles offshore. I finned mostly on the surface, whilst my buddies dived. On the way back, maybe three miles from shore, I jumped off the boat with my raft. and swam back. I missed breakfast, but came ashore happily. It was a fab swim. Laying on the raft and kicking was something I could do all day, so I did.

On returning home, I contacted a boat builder and gave him the idea to build me a solid raft, capable of being carried like a rucksack, but would hold food, water and camping equipment, whilst I laid upon it and kicked, or which I could tow behind me as I swam. If I got into trouble, I could simply get on the raft to rest.

Sea of Cortez, Baja

I named the raft 'Nicola' because every good women should have a boat named after her. She was perfect. MT Solomons had moved to Baja and lived in a retreat on the Sea of Cortez. I took my raft and spent four weeks there. After two or three days doing a few practice swims and some gentle freediving, I packed the raft with as much food and water as it would hold. It was so heavy, I could only drag it across the sand. However, once on the water, not only did it float, but would stay floating even when I lay on it. I waved goodbye to MT, lay on the raft, and started to kick.

I simply swam down the coast. Either kicking, with half my body on the raft, or holding the raft ahead of me or swimming ahead of the raft and towing it. When I got tired I rested on the raft. When night fell, I swam ashore, put up my tent, ate some food and fell asleep. Every beach was deserted, a wilderness, pristine. The beaches were separated by a headland and small sections of cliff. I swam to each headland always keen to get around it to see what lay beyond. Of course it was another beach, maybe one mile across the bay, maybe three or four. I would either swim directly across or hug the coast. I swam down the coast for seven days then turned around to swim back. I ran out of food half way back. Just as Captain Scott had in Antarctica. For ten days I hadn't seen a single person close enough to wave at. I had rigged up a sail on the raft to experiment with. It worked ok, but only directly down wind. Although, with me laying half in the water, it had no speed at all. But when I swam ahead of the raft, it felt as though, at least, it took the weight of the raft. I returned to the retreat after fourteen days of being alone, except near the end when I met a couple American hippies living under the radar, on the beach. Their lifestyle costing them less than one dollar a day.

I knew then, I had found (maybe even invented) a new sport. I researched the internet for other swimmers doing long distance multi day swim journeys and didn't find anything.

I remembered walking the South West Coastal Footpath with Big John, in winter. Saying to him, it would be easier to swim across the bays, rather than hike up and down the cliff around the bay and back up and down the next cliff.

Swimming with the raft, was no different than hiking a long distance coast path. But no one in the world seemed to be doing it. I got home to England after one month of true pioneering adventure and started playing with my raft for the next twenty years. In that time, every now and again I heard of a swimmer taking on a long distance coastline swim, towing their kit.

Jurassic Coast, England

Of course, none of these adventures had happened yet, so let's get back to Taunton, and Nicola, and the boys. I came to terms with having not joined the RAF, nor becoming a missionary, but being a retail jeweller and it all hanged on Nicola. Everything changed thanks to her asking me to marry her.. Everything was worth it because of her.

Back in Taunton, I needed a regular job to get a mortgage, so I contacted the local paper. They made a story of the jeweller who was offering a months wages to an employer who would take him on as a milkman so he could have the rest of the day to build his business. Two dairies offered me a job. I loved being a milkman and the dairy did not want me to give up my first months wages.

We bought the cheapest house in Taunton and started our new life as a milkman and selling our jewellery through party planning, gradually ending with a few ladies doing the same for us in nearby towns.

After a while the work got too much, we were all over the place doing parties, delivering orders and running ourselves ragged. It was time to open our own shop. We had an open day at the house and sold lots of belongings, the music centre, the TV, everything had a price ticket. We even sold the house. We moved around the corner and bought a shop. In the first year of trading we made a profit of £11,000 which was £3,000 more than my salary as a jewellery shop manager. Living above the shop wasn't great but we proved to ourselves that we could make it running our own shop, despite it being one mile from the town centre. We obtained another mortgage and bought a new house to live in.

After a couple years, we started to consider moving the business into town. An established retailer was up for sale and our offer to buy the business was accepted. There was one catch. We had to sell our shop to fund it and this might take too long. It was agreed that Nicola and I would staff the new shop on a salary until our shop was sold. It only took eight weeks to sell and complete. We put the money in the bank and told the owner we were now ready to go to solicitors to buy the business. He said, words to the effect of, sorry but during these few weeks since we started, his brother had sold the last of his three shops (their father, a retired jeweller, had six shops and gave his two sons three shops each). The Taunton shop, Herbert White, was now the last of the six, and he didn't have the heart to tell his father, he had sold the last one. We would have to wait until the father was dead. He was ninety two…….and in any case, he loved what we were doing with the business, it had received a new vitality, his previous manager having just retired at seventy five).

We felt betrayed, having closed our own business and selling the shop, but accepted we had to wait a while. It was ok, we would just keep on running the new shop as if it were our own. Two years later, the owner (working in Canada as a geologist), phoned and said that father was still alive and well, but that they were now ready to sell. There was just one thing, they would only sell 49%.

The price however, would remain the same. I argued that he had effectively doubled the price. He agreed, ending with "but after all, you have doubled the turnover".

I ended the call abruptly and took a walk into town to cool off. I popped into an old school friend's shop to see if he knew of any shops going. He mentioned the old butchers opposite him in St James Street. It was huge and ugly. He suggested I see his landlord who owned a fair few shops in town. His office was just around the corner. I went to see the landlord Brian Haimes, he said he had the old butchers shop and I explained it was too big and would be awkward to convert. He pulled open a drawer, brought out some plans, and unrolled them onto his desk. He had received planning permission to convert the building into three shops. We walked across to have a look inside. It took ten seconds to say yes, we would take the first shop.

I returned to work, and sent a fax to my 'boss' handing in my notice. I then told the landlord we wanted the first two shops of the three. The landlord would do the conversion and we would do the shop fitting. We were trading within four months, in time for Christmas 1991. We sold as much jewellery in the first three months in our new shop as Herbert White took in a year. The third part of the building was let to a locksmiths. They stayed for about three years before relocating to larger premises. We took the opportunity to take their space too, and ended up with the whole building.

Our business had started by selling silver initials door to door after working together for other jewellery retailers for twelve years. We would spend the next thirty five years working together, side by side in our own shops. Eventually opening a second shop in Sidmouth. Then Covid lockdowns forced us to take six months off, and we loved it. So much so, that when the lease expired on Sidmouth, we decided to retire a couple years early. We kind of knew that if we renewed the lease, we would just keep on working for the next ten years. I felt that the ages between sixty five and seventy five were too valuable to spend working. What was the point of keeping on working anyway, just to earn more money at the cost of having less life. We decided we would re-pot our lives and see what would come of it.

St James St, Taunton. 1991. Our first shop in the town centre.

Sidmouth 2019

It was Dad who had shown that we could do these things. To make difficult choices seem straight forward, work with (or blow) the consequences. To take control, be decisive and make it happen. The value of good hard work. Not relying on others but being prepared to take anything on and making it work. To not fear failure. To take the knocks if they come, and learn to lose before you learn to win. To learn to do both and do them well. To be competitive and tough it out when it was time to fight. He caused swimming to be important to me. To be good at something, even to excel at something, even to be the best at something.

That same year in which I won the Chivers trophy when I was sixteen, I was selected by the Air Training Corps to swim 100 yards butterfly and 100 yards freestyle in the National Inter Services Swimming Championships. I won both my races and brought home two marvelous trophies. I took them in to show my fellow cadets at 41F, and my Commanding Officer wanted a photo for the local Gazette. After that was over, I was called into his office. I stepped in, came to attention and snapped the best salute I could. After the usual "Well done, brought good attention to the squadron, inspired the younger cadets", he asked what I had planned for the coming couple of weeks. I said, "I have nothing planned, Sir". He asked me whether I would like to spend a week at an RAF station to attend a glider flying course. Ten days later I took my first few solo flights, got an ATC Wings badge and a couple of stripes. I was sixteen and had experienced something very special. That first solo flight was a very special day.

Cpl Haydn Welch

Slingsby Kirby Cadet Glider

Some weeks later, now old enough to drive, Dad would have me drive to college every day and whenever and wherever he needed to go, I had to drive him. I never had a single proper driving lesson. Before my test, I drove from Taunton to RAF Abingdon for a Canopy Club reunion. I can't remember whether Dad was in a fit state for me to drive him home. I am certain he fell asleep, but what an adventure that was. Truthfully though, the earlier reunions were the best. I remember one time, I just snuck off and wandered on my own amongst the aircraft that were parked some way off the hangar. I walked around them stroking the dope covered camouflage fabric, content just to touch them. Too afraid to get in, but hoping a pilot would come over and ask if I would like to go up.

At one Air Training Corps summer camp, a couple years before my first solo, many cadets had food poisoning on the day allocated for Chipmunk flights. As there were so few cadets able to fly, our slots were extended from twenty minutes to forty minutes each. Once in the air, the pilot handed me control and I flew the aeroplane according to his instructions for the duration. Then coming into land, a Hercules was on the live runway doing engine tests. We were sent away for another thirty minutes. I had the longest flight in the camp. These were special days. Ultimately I bought a Goldwing microlight and every flight was a special day.

Goldwing Microlight

About three months after starting to drive, I had my driving test. Driving out of the test centre I was immediately stuck at the junction trying to turn right onto Station Road. I simply could not get out of the side street onto the road due to the traffic. I couldn't decide whether I was being too cautious and should be more assertive or what to do. It seemed I had to make a decision. Funny thing was that Dad had walked away from the test centre and was standing on the corner watching me. He saw my predicament. So, pretending to be an ordinary pedestrian, he simply started to amble across the road in front of all the traffic. It gave me the perfect opportunity to drive out. The examiner proceeded to take me along the exact route from the test centre through town and beyond college. The same route I had driven probably fifty times before. I felt quite comfortable after that and passed my test first time. Dad had not got back to the test center, so whilst I waited to tell him the news, I peeled the L plates off the car. When Dad arrived he knew I had passed my test when he saw (from a distance) the plates had gone. Dad drove me home.

Now fifty years later, as I write this, I look back at that list of dreams and my 'bucket list' written twenty years before the world ever heard of that phrase. I wish I kept the list. It got to fifty, easily. Then it reached one hundred. There are a whole bunch of things I remember from it and a whole bunch are done. One was to deliver a baby (preferably one belonging to Nicola). It didn't happen. I haven't become an astronaut, neither have I climbed Everest, nor walked to the South Pole. The funny thing is, it seems nowadays, these things can be achieved by anybody with enough money, but for me, that robs the purity of doing them. I don't want to walk to the South Pole because I can afford it (which I can't), I want to do it because it calls me, even though I can't afford it. I realise I am not a mountaineer, nor a polar explorer. I am a swimmer that likes adventures.

My new raft is big enough to sleep in.

There will no doubt be many more adventures as Nicola allows me (with much trepidation sometimes) to feed that rat. Rowing the Atlantic would be a real challenge and I know if I were to make a couple of phone calls, that ball would start rolling, but I also know for sure, I shan't be making those calls. There will always be a whole bunch of other adventures floating around to be seen off, somewhere wet, somewhere soon. Some I know, must just wait until I simply decide they were always going to remain a dream. I am a swimmer without a cause. Dad would be happy with that.

Nowadays Nicola might stay at home, while I go off alone. The request to "Come too" more easily countered, she has spent too many hours on a cold beach waiting for me to swim ashore, or on a desolate airfield waiting for me to land. But she is always waiting for me at home with that gorgeous smile and I am always pleased to get home. I know the best adventure of all is being married to her. Dad would be happy with that too.

Haydn Welch

Lorna: And what of my Dad. Throughout my childhood I was terrified of him, but loved him dearly too and wanted to make him proud of me.

Dad also taught me how to drive, like Haydn, every day I would drive to work and back again, always the long way round, with him beside me. If he wanted to go anywhere, I would drive him there. He was an excellent teacher and I do not remember him every getting frustrated or angry. I passed my driving test on the first attempt, at 17 years and 3 months old. Like Haydn, after passing he drove me home and I never drove him anywhere again.

When I was with him I would normally do exactly what he told me to do. Often that was to be quiet and not to interrupt. Over many years I stayed quiet and did not interrupt, but he never told me not to listen. I find it very strange that a man who was so secretive would forget that his daughter had ears! I would stand behind doors, hide in cupboards, and pretend I was doing other stuff, when in fact I was deliberately eves-dropping. I loved it when my father took us to RAF reunions and open days. My brothers would go off and play on the parachute training equipment, and I would sit quietly beside my dad while he chatted with his RAF mates, pretending to read. I loved the stories they would tell each other. Stories about his CEO and friend called Paddy, about guerilla warfare, spies, espionage and secrets. I couldn't get enough of it. I dared not mention these conversations to my dad or anyone else.

My father's favourite sayings were "Don't talk about it, don't think about it, step over the bodies and do not look back". When he would talk openly about certain wartime activities he would go so far and end the chat with "I can't tell you any more, if I did I would have to kill you".

He hated gossip, and when we told tales on each other he was never pleased. Not only would the other one be punished for whatever they had done, he would also be angry with the informer. So, I learnt quickly to say nothing about any of the 'naughty' things they got up to, or those I did.

On one RAF reunion at Brize Norton, there was a small exhibition of logs and documents on display. There was no one else around and my father was scrolling though one of the log books, when I saw him tear a few pages out of it, fold them up and put them in his pocket. Knowing I had seen him do this he told me that the pages were his and that I must not tell anyone he had taken them. After he died, I was given these pages. They were of a training course held at Kabrit, no. 47 dated 10th June 1943. The logs contained all the details of the trainees. Their name, age, rank, service number, units, dates of descents, the instructors names and comments. The units were from the 11thB, SBS, SAS, 135 FA and No4 and identified my father as the NCO in charge. I returned these papers to the IWM Airborne Forces Archives at Duxford to be reattached to their original logs and was given the opportunity to view them, but not to photograph or take notes. The logs were (and still are) classified. Why he took these, and not any of the other pages he was mentioned in, is unknown.

One of the entries I read was about one particular trainee who failed the course and the reason for the failure, my Dad had written up was "He Died", and no further explanation was given. I often wonder if this chap was the same man my Dad mentioned when I asked him if he had ever killed anyone during the war. His reply was "only one I can be certain of". He went on to say that he had shot at a few Germans/Italians but never went over to check if they were still breathing, and that he had been in a few hand to hand fights and although these men went down, he did not know if they survived or not, with the exception of this one, who he said definitely died.

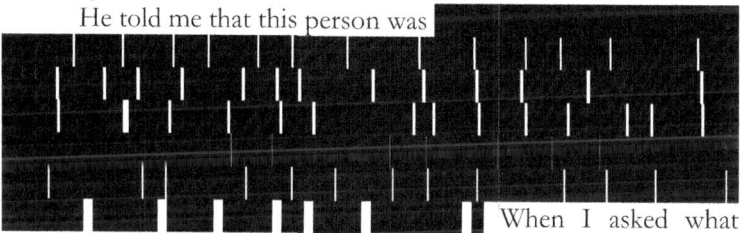

He told me that this person was ▮▮▮▮▮▮▮▮▮▮▮▮▮▮▮▮▮▮▮▮▮▮ When I asked what happened to the other man, he shrugged his shoulders and said "he died too, but it had nothing to do with me". **Lorna Welch**

Haydn: One late night, Dad arrived h0me with blood all over his shirt, none of which belonged to him. It seems upon arriving at Bridgwater and after unlocking the studio, but before he had time to switch on the lights, he was jumped on from behind………………..Suffice to say, the burglar argued with the police that Dad had been a little too rough. Also suffice to say, you should never grab an old man from behind. He might just have served in the desert with the SAS.

Another late night, or rather, early morning, Dad came into my bedroom to wake me up and told me to get dressed. It was 3am. He needed to show me something. We got into the car and drove to Vivary Park in Taunton. There we found Fred Jago who was walking around the park attempting to break the World Record for the longest non-stop walk. Dad explained that these early hours were the toughest and there was no point in cheering him on in the day, it would be now that he needed the encouragement. We stayed about an hour. Fred broke the record after 116 hours and walking 304 miles. Some twenty years or so later, in 1991, Dad turned up at a similar time in the morning to swim alongside me when I attempted a 24 hour swim at my local gym.

I had decided as part of my English Channel swim training to see if I could at least swim the distance in a pool, so challenged myself to try a 24 hour swim. When the time was up, I had covered 42 miles. Dad helped me out of the pool and was unusually attentive. I felt fine, but to all accounts I did not look it. Unbeknown to me, the gym owners had doubled the chlorine content in the pool (assuming I would pee in it). The chlorine had burnt all the hair off my entire body. The fine hairs on my arms and legs were completely stripped. The hair on my head had frazzled to small pills of fluff much like the surface of a woollen jumper, and had turned an unusual pale green. During the swim, at the end of each hour I remember having a drink and running my hands through my hair. I had noticed how smooth it all felt and put it down to the wrinkles forming on my fingertips affecting my touch sensation. I even mentioned it a couple of times. Of course, my support team were aware and quite concerned to see it happening but kept it a secret. Dad held me up as we walked to the changing room. I had no idea why. Then I removed my Speedos and was surprised to find I looked twelve years old again, I knew something unusual had happened.

When I got home and after having had a good sleep, I phoned Dr Penny, the swimming club doctor. Although my mouth was sore, I did not feel unwell. I just knew he would be fascinated about my hair loss. With the chlorine burns and bald head, I looked like I was a cancer survivor. Dr Penny was writing a paper about medical conditions swimmers experienced and was fascinated. He came over straight away. I gave him permission to take a few photographs, he promised to edit them so I would remain anonymous. A few days later, I had my visit with Brian Haimes, and maybe the way I looked after that swim proved to him I was able to see important plans through, and convinced him to allow me to take the lease of the shop.

Fred's walking records and Dad wanting to support him may have been inspired a decade or so earlier in 1959 and 1960 by RAF PJI Patrick Moloney. Moloney held records for walking John O'Groats to Land's End in 18 days, St David's Head to Lowestoft in 5 days, Edinburgh to London in 6 days, San Francisco to New York (3032 miles) in 66 days and Londonderry to Cork in 4 days. Detailed in his book, 'I Never Walked Alone'.

In the late 70s, Saturday Night Fever brought the youngsters to the studio, Dad would hold disco dances for under 16s at Taunton. One night a group of Hell's Angels wanted to be allowed in. Well, that was never going to happen. They returned a couple weeks later. It was then the offer was suggested by one brave soul to take the argument into the toilets..........well that was an offer Dad could not refuse. There was Mum, my sister Lorna and her husband Tony, plus five Hell's Angels huddled at the top of the stairs. After quite some battering and clashing around with a fair few groans and much yelling, out came a rather dejected and broken 6' 2" twenty something, supported by the arms of Dad who (now an OAP) was sporting his rather cocky grin. Dad did say he was a good opponent and threw some good punches. The Hell's Angels agreed that if Dad ever needed any 'help' he just needed to contact them.

Haydn Welch

Lorna remembers the back story:

Lorna: My brother has already mentioned the time he took a Hell's Angel chap into the dance school's toilet block. I was there at the time. This event was preceded by another. A few weeks earlier, at the under 18's regular Friday night "Northern Soul" dance parties (not a Saturday Night Fever disco), a gang of Hell's Angels tried to gain entrance to the event. Both of my parents and I were at the door when they attempted to barge in. One of them pushed past my mother (who was thrown against the stairs) and came face to fist with my father. Just one punch, and this chap went flying backward onto the rest of the gang who had not quite passed the threshold. The whole group tumbled backwards, such was the force of the 'flying angel'. With 90% of this man now outside, with just his lower leg still inside the building, my father slammed the heavy doors shut. By goodness, did the chappie scream! My father then opened the door to kick his now broken leg out of the building, closing and locking the doors behind him. Both the police and ambulance arrived and my father was arrested and placed on bail pending further enquiries. The Hell's Angel chap did not press charges, that was not their way preferring to deal with these matters themselves, and the case was dropped. They had turned up two weeks later to get justice in their own way, it didn't work out too well for them then either. On a sub note, the chap my father took into the toilets became a regular weekly visitor as did their 'boxing spars' and this chap ensured that his gang knew that the Dancing School was a 'protected' place.

Lorna Welch

Haydn: Another evening during a private lesson in Taunton (the studio being above a late night bar), loud music rising through the floor from the club below and making it hard for Dad to teach, drowning out the mellow sound of Englebert Humpledink's "The Last Waltz" coming from dads gramophone………….After the lesson concluded, Dad fetched a sledge hammer and a block of wood from a storeroom, placed the wood on the centre of the dance floor and commenced bashing it hard, with the hammer. It didn't take long for the manager of the club to arrive upstairs with Dad still banging away. The story goes, that as Dad approached the man now at his door, Dad 'tripped' over his feet whilst carrying the sledge hammer. The bar manager saw it differently. It didn't get to court, but I believe the police commandeered the sledgehammer.

Another 'incident' occurred when Nicola and I returned to Taunton to start our own retail jewellery business. Having sold our house in Eastbourne some weeks earlier, we had now exchanged contracts on a house in Taunton. During this time we (along with our pre-school boys Ben and Joe) had taken to camping in the front room of the bungalow at Eastwick Avenue with Mum and Dad. It really wasn't suitable so we had asked the local Council if they had anywhere more suitable for the few weeks between exchange and completion. Whilst I was at work, Nicola and Dad were visited by a social worker to check over the living arrangements.

Dad immediately scowled at the young lady and in no uncertain terms, yelled in her face to get us out of the house. The dog, a German Shepherd, did not like the confrontation and wanted to get involved. Dad kicked the dog and bellowed at it to 'go away', the dog yelped and left the scene. Nicola of course, being aware of Dad, but not especially being used to him, did not have to act afraid, it showed in her eyes. As the social worker was leaving she simply said to her "You can see what it is like having to live here". When the front door closed behind this young lady, Dad smiled at Nicola and with a smile on his face and a wink in his eye said, "All right Nic?" "You b*****d!" was the reply. We were rehoused into self-contained emergency housing within a couple of days, until we moved into our new home four weeks later.

The thing is with Dad, all these 'Boys Own' episodes (even the punishments) were acts. During the moments before and after them, he was his normal charming controlled self. When he needed to be the military version of himself he just flicked that switch on, did what he did then switched it off again.

I wish I could sit Dad down and talk things over. Not just to hear the stories one more time but to ask questions, of which there are many. The boxing match with Bruce Woodcock for instance. I was able to obtain a copy of Bruce's ghostwritten biography hoping for answers and to find out more of his war wars. Why was Bruce on the Windsor Castle? Bruce was never called up as he had a protected job as an engineer, he was required to stay in England to build trains. Bruce only left England to fight in Ireland. Is it really possible the fight might have occurred between Liverpool and Dublin? Would Bruce really have risked a fight with Dad (who was the current inter services boxing champion) during a rough and short voyage whilst feeling sea sick? More importantly, would he have fought Dad whilst on his way to an International boxing competition in Ireland, representing England as the current ABA champion? Was fellow "Toff" Jim Averis 'wrong' to suggest phrases like 'tropical heat'. Maybe a cover story was in the making. And why did "The Toffs" disembark at Freetown anyway? It was rather a long way from Kabrit.

Haydn Welch

Lorna sheds more light (or maybe even some shadows) onto these questions:

Lorna: I have been actively researching my father's war time years. It has been a long hard struggle, going down so many rabbit holes and coming to so many dead ends or ends that make no sense. I have read most of the reports and books on the subject of how the SAS were formed and the early days of the Ringway Parachute Training School.

I was also with my father at home, when the SAS stormed the Iranian Embassy and secured the release of the hostages. I was with him a few years later when Stirling and ten of the SAS 'Originals' talked about their experiences in a self-made documentary filmed in 1984 during a reunion. This was broadcast just once and did not resurface for another thirty five years, when it was used to produce the BBC documentary SAS Rogue Warriors by Ben Macintyre, with the BBC saying these clips are being broadcast for the first time. I know that to be untrue.

When the original full version was broadcast in 1984/85, my father went wild. This was the first time I realised that the stories I had heard, and overheard, were about the SAS.

Beforehand he said he worked alongside L Detachment and the LRDG. During the showing he got very angry and told me not to believe a word that came out of Stirling's mouth, and when the 'Originals' told their story he shouted at the TV saying "which bit of 'don't talk about it' did you not understand". Come the end he reached for his whisky glass, a sign I would normally take as my time to make a withdrawal. I was in my mid-twenties and was no longer terrified by him. I took the opportunity to get further details of many raids he had taken part in. When I asked him why he was not mentioned (and never was in the many subsequent books), he said without any of his previous humorous tones "I was not meant to be there, and if any of them mention my name, what I did, or give any indications of my presence, not only will I ensure they say nothing ever again, they will be breaking the Official Secrets Act and will face extreme punishment one way or the other". Ending our chat with, "I am sorry I really cannot say any more and remember you must not talk about this or repeat anything you have heard tonight". I promised I wouldn't and he said "I know, you are a good'un", and for my dad that was the highest compliment he could give anyone.

My father did not lie, he would however muddy the waters, and the clearer they are becoming the more I am certain that my father was a damned sight more than a Parachute Instructor. He was a man of his time, a man who believed that secrets should remain secrets. He always said that during WWII he felt more alive than he has ever done, they were the best times of his life and nothing he has done, or will do, could come close to that.

In the last years of my father's life, dementia slowly took hold. Denise and Rachel did everything they could to keep him at home. He was still remarkably strong, and therefore a danger to himself and others. He had always been clear on how he wanted to leave this world—by taking one final hike to a quiet spot by the river, where he would rest in peace, with strict instructions that no one should come looking for him. "Go to the pub and have a drink until it's over," he would tell me, ever the pragmatist.

One day, I think he truly decided enough was enough. He set off on his own and was later found sitting beside the River Tone, very much alive and defiant. Shortly after, he developed pneumonia and was transferred to the hospital. We braced ourselves for the inevitable, but Dad had other plans. He fought that virus with every bit of his strength, winning his final battle, and was transferred to a lovely hospice for his last weeks

There's one last story I'd like to share. Fifteen days before he passed, we celebrated his 89th birthday. I usually bought him a large bottle of whiskey, but this year I brought a miniature. I knew he wasn't allowed to have it, but rules were made to be broken.

As I approached him, he looked at me with a faint, blank expression, wondering, Who on earth is this?

"Hi, Dad," I said softly, leaning in. "Happy birthday."

He blinked, squinting as if trying to place me.

"Oh," he murmured. "Is it my birthday?" After a moment, he looked up with a glimmer of recognition, and managed, "You're a good'un, aren't you?"

"That's right, Dad. I'm a good'un."

His smile grew, and then, as if letting me in on a secret, he leaned closer and asked, "Are you here to get me out of this place?"

In his mind, he wasn't in a nursing home; he was a prisoner of war. He explained how the "guards" insisted he take "drugs" that left him foggy, and when he refused, they forced him. Without missing a beat, I opened the miniature bottle, poured it into his empty teacup, and handed it to him, saying, "This should make you feel a lot better." He couldn't hold the cup, so I helped him take a sip. When I tried to take it away, he slurped loudly and finished every last drop.

Then he sat back, silent for a moment, before saying, as clear as day, "Is Paddy with you?"

"Yes, Dad," I replied. "And so is Ian."

Paddy and Ian had been close friends, though Paddy had never quite recovered from losing Ian during Operation Squatter.

Dad's face lit up, and he said, "Get on!"

"Yes, they're both waiting for you. The others are with them too." I said.

He seemed so energized, asking about the plan, how he would know when to move, and what he needed to do to help. Caught off guard, I told him his part was to play along, to act like a model inmate—charming, cooperative, and most importantly, to take the meds and eat as much as possible.

He grumbled, frustrated by the confusion the pills caused, but I reassured him.

"As soon as you're free, we have an antidote. Everything will be okay, but the mission depends on you following orders exactly. Do you understand, Joe?" I asked, deliberately using his call sign.

Grinning, he replied, "Yes, I understand. I'll be a good boy." Then, with a twinkle in his eye, he asked, "Have you got any more tea?"

"No more tea, Dad," I replied. "If you had more, they'd catch on."

"Yes," he nodded. "I understand. I'll be ready. What will the signal be?"

For a moment, I wondered if I should keep going. But his happiness made it easy to decide. For the next hour, he drifted in and out of "being with me." Sometimes, I followed what he was saying; other times, I couldn't.

He often said, "Do you remember X and when we did Y?" Each time, I said I did, asking him for stories or messages to pass on. Eventually, a nurse came over, gently reminding us it was time for him to rest. As I leaned in to kiss him goodbye, he looked at me and said,

"You're Lorna, aren't you?"

"Yes, Dad," I replied.

"I knew you were," he said. "I know a good'un when I see one."

"Yes, you do, Dad."

He smiled and asked, "Will I see you before the off?"

"Oh, yes. I'll come back soon and let you know the next steps. Remember, you must be a good boy. Can you do that?"

"For you, I'd do anything," he said with a smile.

And that was our last conversation. He was happy, caught up in our shared illusion, still the resilient man he'd always been.

He passed away on March 30, 2007. While I waited for the news of his passing, I honored his wishes and had that drink—or, if I'm honest, quite a few.
Rest in Peace Dad, you too are a good'un and I am proud to be your daughter.

Father made my history
He fought for what he thought would somehow set us free
He taught me what to say in school
I learn it off by heart, but now that's torn in two

(Spandou Ballet, Through the Barricades 1986)

Lorna Welch

Haydn: One day, Dad now eighty four years old, popped into our jewellery shop in Taunton. Smartly dressed in his RAF blazer, wings proudly displayed above his breast pocket. My wife Nicola asked him where he had been, it looked like he had been to a funeral. Dad said, "No, a wedding". "Whose wedding?" Nicola asked. "Mine", Dad replied.

Time gently passed and work got in the way of life. I can't remember exactly when we realised that Dad was getting old. We thought he would live forever. He would often pop into the shop to say hello, we would have a laugh and a natter. Maybe he was shuffling more than usual, and sometimes we had to tune in to how he was speaking. Then one day he declared with some passion, that he was going back into the air force. The trouble is, I never assumed that Dad would get ever get old. Right up until then he was still teaching. Nobody could touch him on the dance floor. He was unstoppable teaching Ballroom, Latin, Disco and American Line Dancing. Everybody who saw him at work recognised he was pretty special.

    Another day, we collected him from his house so Denise could have the day off. We brought him to ours and sat him in a comfy chair and talked over a whole lot of things. Nicola and I spoke of the war, the dancing school and Mum. It seemed he remembered her but had forgotten he was once married to her. Although he said she was a good'un. We reminded him that she was my mother, and I was his son. "Get on!" He said. He needed help going to the loo and far too soon became agitated wondering where he was and why Denise was not with him. We took him home earlier than we would have liked. It was surprising but he really did seem to be getting old.

    Dad spent his last few weeks in a hospice and even then I thought he was there for respite rather than end of life care. We would natter as usual. He seemed rather bored of it all and looked tired (as all do who are forced to lay in bed for too many days). It didn't occur to me at all that he was dying, but would be up and about in a few days.

    Then I got a call and didn't have much time. I arrived at the hospice and met Denise who had been there a fair while. She had said her goodbyes already and was about to leave Dad with his family. It seemed wrong to be there with him and Denise having gone home. She was his family too.

    For maybe thirty minutes it was just me and my dad. I sat by his bed and held his hand. He may have been aware, or not. But I talked with him anyway and hoped he could still hear despite his morphine induced stupor. His face was not ravaged by the years, maybe a little thin, not gaunt, but as rugged as always it was. I held his hands in mine. Mine fitted into his as a child's hand would fit into their fathers. I folded them into a fist. Gosh, they still looked fearsome. They seemed to symbolise his life. Strong and powerful for a boxer yet when opened, they were gentle and precise to support and direct his dance partner. I wished they had cuddled me more often. I wished they had ruffled my hair more often. I wished they had stroked my forehead more often. I wished they had been placed on my head to gently bless me. I looked at my hands looking so small compared to his. Mine had got me across the English Channel, twice, so they weren't so bad and Dad for sure would have recognised that. I looked at them again and realised that whilst his hands had never blessed me, neither had mine blessed him and there was little time to make that right.

    I gently placed my hands on his head and spoke with him. I let him know he was loved, that I was honoured to be his son. That it was ok to be a little nervous of the future but that it would be an exciting journey. To watch out for his family, his loved ones and his friends. I said other things that needed to be said and he tried to respond. I couldn't tell if he was grumbling or thanking me for sharing a prayerful moment.

    I sat back down and stroked his brow just as my older sister Juliet and Len (her husband) arrived then Mark my older brother turned up. Lorna was not going to make it. Within a couple minutes, my one to one with Dad had finished. I wished I'd have had many more of them. I sat back to let the others speak with him.

    Dad's breathing seemed fairly slow. I slipped my hand under the covers and rested one under his rib cage. I could feel him breathe in and breathe out, there would then be a short pause before I felt a gentle flutter and he took another breath in. After a few minutes, the pause between breaths seemed to take longer whilst remaining peaceful and not forced, as though he was sleeping. A slow breath in, a passive exhalation followed by nothing for twenty seconds, then a gentle flutter from his diaphragm and another breath. My freedive training told me all I needed to know. After maybe ten minutes, the pause between breaths became longer. It was amazing. His empty lung 'breath holding' extended from twenty seconds to one minute, then longer still. I thought that each breath had to be his last, such was the time he was taking between breaths. Then another flutter and another breath. We started to remark that we thought he had gone, and a minute or so later he would take one more peaceful breath. We started to 'tell him off', saying we were all there, all holding his hand, all caring for him and all allowing him to go. Each pause between breaths we thought was his last. A minute passed plus a little longer, yet the flutter came and he took one more. For thirty minutes, my hand stayed resting on his abdomen throughout.

I was looking at his peaceful face noticing tiny red capillaries in the lids of his closed eyes. Then during the quiet spell between breaths, waiting to feel the flutter and the next breath, Dad's eyelids went grey in a single moment. I knew he had already taken his last breath.

When the time came, there was no urgent call to "Action Stations", no word "GO" bellowed in Dad's face. He wasn't pushed, and he certainly didn't fall. In a moment of complete relaxation and peace, he simply stood in the door, closed his eyes, jumped and was gone.

Before Dad went into hospital, his wife Denise took him to see her dentist. Upon checking his teeth, the dentist remarked that he had never seen a cyanide drilling before, he had only heard about them.

Now, that's another story begging to be told……………..

Haydn Welch

15 THE PJIs

The PJIs whose anecdotes have filled these pages are listed. Including of course Winston Churchill even though he wasn't one, but as he is quoted in the first paragraph he belongs here too, as none of this would have happened without him.

"The Four Toffs", I thank my sister Lorna (Lorie Randell) who corrected some of my memories, added some lovely information and who has done much work of her own in researching these fine men. To the families of "The Four Toffs", there is a book there waiting to be written, along with Dad's cyanide drilling I look forward to reading all about it.

I must thank again Julie Hearn, Peter's daughter for happily allowing Peter's document to be fully published for all who might now find it. And most of all Peter, upon whom this book has relied. For his collection of previously unpublished anecdotes, received from the many Parachute Jump Instructors contributing these tales.

The first eight chapters (as given to me in that old type written document twenty years ago) are his work, copied exactly from his original writings (along with a few additions and the images which I have inserted along the way.

It seems Peter gave one or two others a similar permission and a few of these anecdotes being reproduced in their works. There remains possibly a handful of A4 sized photocopies of Peter's original typewritten document, with its faded blue paper cover held in archives, museums or personal collections around the world. I hope Peter will be pleased to see these musings in book form, now published in their fullness, inspiring others to jump and do the other things.

Peter was one of the last of his breed of pioneers, the last of an original group of people who learnt how to jump by the seat of their pants, by trial and error and then by trial and error sought to teach the troops to do the same. He was one who started to bring the stories of these Parachute Jump Instructors to light, these pioneers, these history makers, these whose names are largely unknown, even sidelined.

Through their work these men have created a parachuting heritage. The stuff of legend. The men who wore parachutes to work, the men who taught the men to jump. Their stories deserve to be told and their names deserve to be remembered.

Terry Allen	Geoff Greenland	John Savill
Harold Appleby	Peter Hearn	John Saxby
Jim Averis	Bill Jevons	Ron Smith
Jimmy Blythe	Stan Kellaway	Louis Strange
Leo Brown	John Mace	Ron Tarry
George Bruce	Natch Markwell	Peter Tingle
Peter Burgess	Nolan May	Maurice Todhunter
Alf Card	Roy McCluskey	Gerry Turnbull
Eddie Cartner	Jake McLoughlin	Val Valentine
Winston Churchill	Reg McNeil	Harry Ward
Johnny Dawes	Erroll Minter	Ernie Warren
Harry Feigen	Ron Mitchell	Peter Watson
Bill Fell	Maurice Newnham	Ken 'Joe' Welch
Liam Forde	Olly Owen	Peter Williams
Jock Fox	Geordie Platts	Jimmy Young
Richard Gale	George Podevin	
Norman Goodacre	Stan Roe	

16 FURTHER READING

Gerald BOWMAN	Jump For It
Edward CARTNER	Jumping Beans
Edward CARTNER	I Have Control
Peter HEARN	Falcons
Peter HEARN	Flying Rebel
Peter HEARN	Parachutist
Peter HEARN	The Sky People
Peter HEARN	Sky High Irvin
Peter HEARN	When the 'Chute Went Up
Damien LEWIS	SAS Brothers in Arms
John LUCAS	The Silken Canopy
Ian MacKERSEY	Into the Silk
Eoin McGONIGAL	Special Forces Brothers in Arms
Peter MORAN	A Speck in the Sky
John NEAL	Bless You Brother Irvin
Maurice NEWNHAM	Prelude to Glory
Louis STRANGE	Recollections of an Airman
John TRANUM	Nine Lives
Harry WARD / Peter HEARN	The Yorkshire Birdman
Dumbo WILLANS	Panic Takes Time
Anon	Parachutist Pegasus 1943

17 ABOUT THE AUTHOR

Group Captain Peter G Hearn BA, AFC, RAF (R'td) 1932 – 2021

Peter Hearn enjoyed his National Service so much he decided to stay on and join the RAF in 1956 as a Physical Training Instructor before progressing as a Parachute Jumping Instructor. Eventually becoming the Commanding Officer of the Parachute Training School.

He founded the RAF Falcons parachute display team. In 1960 he represented Great Britain in the World Parachuting Championships. Peter served in the SAS and with the Far East Jungle Rescue Team. Retiring from the RAF in 1987 with the rank of Group Captain. He received the Air Force Cross and the Queen's Commendation for Valuable Service in the Air.

He is an accomplished author of several parachuting themed books including The Sky People, along with biographical books of other aviation and parachute pioneers including Sky High Irvin, When the 'Chute Went Up and Flying Rebel. He has also written three fictional novels.

ABOUT THE AUTHOR

Haydn Welch flew solo before he was old enough to drive solo. He walked the Pennine Way aged 16 with two friends. Subsequently spending the rest of his teenage years and early 20s jumping out of aeroplanes, hang gliding and paragliding, eventually settling for flying a Goldwing microlight.

He and his wife Nicola opened a retail jewellery shop in Taunton in 1991 whilst Haydn returned to his first love of swimming. Later opening a second shop in Sidmouth. He swam the English Channel in 1992. Only to return again in 1993 becoming the first person in the world to swim the English Channel backstroke in a time of 17 hours 2 minutes.

In 1994, having swam the width of the Channel twice, Haydn attempted to swim the length of the Channel from Dover to Lands' End (wearing just his Speedos, cap and goggles). He abandoned the swim due to gales, after swimming sometimes alone, sometimes escorted by his son Joe in a RIB, 200 miles in three weeks. Sleeping on the beach or in a tent while Nicola drove the support vehicle.

After these swims, Haydn looked for a more recreational sport and started freediving. In 2002, Haydn held the British record for Dynamic Apnea by swimming 139 meters underwater on just one breath. He represented England at The Pacific Cup in Hawaii where he completed a distance of 156 meters but was disqualified after being judged too close to unconsciousness. The winner covering 150 meters and the current World Record holder Herbert Nitsch 144 meters.

Returning to open water swimming, in 2013 he swam an official Ice Mile, one mile in 3.7 degree water temperature, again wearing just his Speedos. Before this swim, he had to wait half the day until the ice sheet melted at Lake Bled.

A member of The Church of Jesus Christ of Latter-day Saints, he and his wife Nicola are now retired and live in the Somerset countryside. Haydn is still swimming rather long distances and Nicola won't let him make another parachute jump.

All I ask is the stoutest task

And a high wide sky above me

And nine good men for a stick of ten

And a girl at home to love me

And a clean jump through

And a landing true.

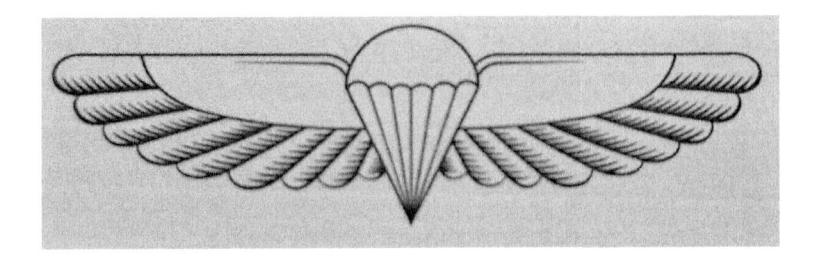

IMAGE CREDITS

Pge	Per Ardua Ad Astra : MoD
iv	Ken Welch : Haydn Welch
08	Louis Strange, Martinsyde : Rebellion
10	Louis Strange : Courtesy ptsheritage.com
11	Whitley Exit : Piemags/Alamy Stock Photo
17	Harry Ward : The Northfield Collection / Asstd Newspapers
19	Tatton Park Balloon : Piemags/ww2archive/AlamyStockPhoto
20	Tatton Park Balloon : Courtesy ptsheritage.com
22	Tatton Park Balloon : SuperStock / Alamy Stock Photo
23	Tatton Park Balloon : Courtesy ptsheritage.com
24	Tatton Park Balloon : Courtesy ptsheritage.com
26	Maurice Newnham : Courtesy ptsheritage.com
26	Prelude to Glory : Haydn Welch
26	Maurice Newnham : Public Domain
28	Joe S/Harry W : Piemags/ww2archive/AlamyStockPhoto
28	WAAF Parachute Packing : Heritage Image Partnership/ASP
30	Down To Tea : Fox Photos/Sydney Morning Herald/Alamy
36	Whitley Exit : Piemags/archive/Military/AlamyStockPhoto
38	Through the Hole : Piemags/ww2archive/AlamyStockPhoto
43	Short Sterling : DeLuan/Alamy Stock Photo
50	Sir Richard Gale : Piemags/ww2archive/AlamyStockPhoto
53	Consolidated B-24 Liberator : GLarchive/AlamyStockPhoto
55	Vickers Wellington : Public Domain
57	Gay Gibson : PA Images/Alamy Stock Photo
61	Lockheed Hudson : Vintage Mechanics/Alamy Stock Photo

62 Bruce Woodcock : B.Woodcock Jr/Hutchinson's Library
63 Ken Welch : Haydn Welch
64 SAS Exit Training : Piemags/ww2archive/AlamyStockPhoto
65 SAS Wings : Anon
66 Bob Tait : Anon
67 Ted Badger/Bob Tait : Anon
67 SAS Crest : Panther Media GmbH/AlamyStockPhoto
68 Ken Welch, Kabrit : Piemags/ww2archive/AlamyStockPhoto
71 Alf Card : Courtesy Graeme Card
73 Douglas Dakota : DeLuan/Alamy Stock Photo
74 Water Buffalo : Public Domain
82 Poker Hand : Public Domain
85 C-82 Fairchild Packett : PJF Military Collection/AlamyStock
86 J C Kilkenny : Courtesy ptsheritage.com
89 Andy Capp : Reg Smythe/Daily Mirror/Public Domain
91 de Havilland Rapide : EY74DT/Alamy Stock Photo
92 de Havilland Tiger Moth : Oskar A. Johansen
97 English Electric Canberra : Chronicle. Alamy Stock Photo
99 Freefall Group Photo : Courtesy Julie Hearn
102 Skydiving Santa : Courtesy Julie Hearn
103 Rolling Stones : Public Domain
105 Triumph TR2 : Public Domain
109 Armstrong Whitworth Argosy : Chronicle/AlamyStockPhoto
116 Peter Hearn/Doug Peacock : Rays Willis / ptsheritage.com
124 Handley Page Victor/Hercules : PA Images AlamyStockPhoto

127 Peter Hearn AFC : Courtesy Julie Hearn
129 Peter Hearn : Courtesy Julie Hearn
132 Ken Welch, Pegasus : Imperial War Museum
135 Haydn/Nicola : Haydn Welch
138 Ken Welch, Pegasus : Imperial War Museum
139 Big John : Haydn Welch
142 Who's the Daddy? : Haydn Welch
147 Dad/Mum Wedding : Haydn Welch
148 RMS Windsor Castle : Anon
149 The Four Toffs, Kabrit : Haydn Welch
150 The Four Toffs, Brize Norton : Haydn Welch
152 Ken Welch, Kabrit : Courtesy Averis
153 David Sterling/Paddy Maine : Public Domain
154 Bristol Bombay : Alamy Stock Photo
155 Ken Welch, Kabrit : Piemags/archive/Military/AlamyStock
157 Ken/Pat : Haydn Welch
158 Ken/Pat : Haydn Welch
158 Dancing School : Sarah Smith/Creative Commons Licence
159 Haydn : Haydn Welch
164 Lorna/Haydn : Haydn Welch
169 Dirty Dancing : Public Domain
172 Goat : Haydn Welch
174 Ken/Juliet, Swanage : Courtesy Juliet Eden
177 Ken/Denise, Corfu : Courtesy Denise Welch
179 Chambers/Howe Trophies : Haydn Welch

181 Same Boy Different Trophies : Haydn Welch
186 Rogallo Hang Glider : Haydn Welch
188 Haydn : Haydn Welch
189 Nicola : Haydn Welch
191 Joe/Ben : Haydn Welch
192 Haydn, English Channel : Courtesy Tom Watch
195 Sea of Cortez : Haydn Welch
197 Jurassic Coast : Haydn Welch
200 Haydn Welch Jewellers, Taunton : Haydn Welch
200 Haydn Welch Jewellers, Sidmouth : Haydn Welch
201 Air Cadet Wings badge : Haydn Welch
202 Haydn Welch, ATC : Haydn Welch
202 Kirby Cadet Glider : CPC Collection/Alamy Stock Photo
203 ATC Wings Badge : Haydn Welch
204 Goldwing Microlight : Haydn Welch
205 Raft : Haydn Welch
225 Knowledge Dispels Fear : Ministry of Defence
226 Vibirus Audax, Bold in Strength : Ministry of Defence
227 Venture Adventure : Ministry of Defence
228 Per Ardua Ad Astra, Through Adversity to the Stars : MoD

Printed in Great Britain
by Amazon